University
of Michigan
Business
School Management Series

INNOVATIVE SOLUTIONS TO THE PRESSING PROBLEMS OF BUSINESS

The mission of the University of Michigan Business School Management Series is to provide accessible, practical, and cutting-edge solutions to the most critical challenges facing business-people today. The UMBS Management Series provides concepts and tools for people who seek to make a significant difference in their organizations. Drawing on the research and experience of faculty at the University of Michigan Business School, the books are written to stretch thinking while providing practical, focused, and innovative solutions to the pressing problems of business.

Executive Summary

This book is for managers who have responsibility for the success of their organizations. It's about discovering competitive advantage in the legal challenges of doing business—discovering, for example, how a lawsuit against your firm can help you develop more profitable products and practices, and how governmental restrictions might actually work to your firm's advantage. In other words, this book can help you to revolutionize your business strategies related to law.

At the heart of this book is the Manager's Legal Plan, a four-step process by which you can not only better defend against costly and wasteful litigation but can actually turn your legal resources into competitive assets. The four steps are as follows:

- *Step One: Understand the law.* This goes beyond the immediate legal challenge and involves more than calling the desperate meetings that managers often have with their lawyers when someone threatens to sue. It involves a broader process of legal education for managers aimed at preventing future litigation while also expanding managers' understanding of the legal terrain.

- *Step Two: React to legal problems through flight or fight.* That is, determine whether conventional legal approaches can be used to resolve your legal concerns. This step is where managers often stop when they try to cope with legal problems: choices among fighting or settling cases, moving the business to another state or country, or possibly seeking legal reforms. The book will explain how increasing globalization of law is greatly reshaping these choices.
- *Step Three: Develop business strategies and solutions to prevent legal problems.* Here legal solutions take a backseat to business solutions. For example, once a wrongful discharge lawsuit has been resolved, the company's hiring practices should be reviewed, company documents should be revised, and employees should receive training that will prevent them from making statements that could result in liability.
- *Step Four: Climb to the balcony to reframe legal concerns as business concerns.* This takes us well beyond the usual business responses to legal challenges. The balcony represents a broader perspective—an overview that can help you to see that what you originally thought was a legal problem in fact represents a broader business opportunity that may enable you to gain new competitive advantage.

Chapter One presents the Manager's Legal Plan in detail. The next three chapters provide examples of how it is used. Each chapter deals with one of your company's stakeholder groups: customers, employees, and society at large (represented by government).

Chapter Two deals with customers, emphasizing product liability lawsuits and new product opportunities arising from such litigation.

Chapter Three deals with employees, especially workers' compensation, wrongful discharge, and sexual harassment concerns. The chapter suggests how the changing nature of employment relationships can help you retain the talented people on whom success depends.

Chapter Four deals with government. The chapter shows, for example, how even stringent environmental regulations can create opportunities for competitive advantage.

Chapter Five addresses a wide variety of supportive legal strategies. Three principal topics are: ensuring that you have the best legal resources and are maximizing their value to you; applying the best available management tools for resolving disputes; and using the Manager's Legal Plan to encourage ethical decision making within your company.

Using the Law for Competitive Advantage

George J. Siedel

JOSSEY-BASS
A Wiley Company
www.josseybass.com

Published by

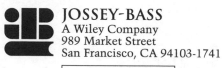

JOSSEY-BASS
A Wiley Company
989 Market Street
San Francisco, CA 94103-1741

www.josseybass.com

Jossey-Bass books and products are available through most bookstores. To contact
Jossey-Bass directly, call (888) 378-2537, fax to (800) 605-2665, or visit our website
at www.josseybass.com.

Substantial discounts on bulk quantities of Jossey-Bass books are available to corporations, professional associations, and other organizations. For details and discount information, contact the special sales department at Jossey-Bass.

We at Jossey-Bass strive to use the most environmentally sensitive paper stocks available to us. Our publications are printed on acid-free recycled stock whenever possible,
and our paper always meets or exceeds minimum GPO and EPA requirements.

Library of Congress Cataloging-in-Publication Data

Siedel, George J.
   Using the law for competitive advantage/George J. Siedel.
      p. cm.—(University of Michigan Business School
management series)
Includes bibliographical references and index.
   ISBN 0-7879-5623-6
   1. Business law—United States. 2. Industrial
management—United States. 3. Competition—United States.
I. Title. II. Series.
   KF390.B84 S56   2002
   346.7307—dc21

2001008352

FIRST EDITION
HB Printing   10 9 8 7 6 5 4 3 2 1

Contents

To my sister, Karen E. Braaten,
and to the memory of my father,
George Joseph Siedel (1912–2001)

Series Foreword

Welcome to the University of Michigan Business School Management Series. The books in this series address the most urgent problems facing business today. The series is part of a larger initiative at The University of Michigan Business School (UMBS) that ties together a range of efforts to create and share knowledge through conferences, survey research, interactive and distance training, print publications, and new media

It is just this type of broad-based initiative that sparked my love affair with UMBS in 1984. From the day I arrived I was enamored with the quality of the research, the quality of the MBA program, and the quality of the Executive Education Center. Here was a business school committed to new lines of research, new ways of teaching, and the practical application of ideas. It was a place where innovative thinking could result in tangible outcomes.

The UMBS Management Series is one very important outcome, and it has an interesting history. It turns out that every year five thousand participants in our executive program fill out a marketing survey in which they write statements indicating the most important problems they face. One day Lucy Chin, one of our administrators, handed me a document containing all these statements. A content analysis of the data resulted in a list of forty-five pressing problems. The topics ranged from growing a company to managing personal stress. The list covered a wide territory, and I started to see its potential. People in organizations tend to be driven by a very traditional set of problems, but the solutions evolve. I went to my friends at Jossey-Bass to discuss a publishing project. The discussion eventually grew into the University of Michigan Business School Management Series— Innovative Solutions to the Pressing Problems of Business.

The books are independent of each other, but collectively they create a comprehensive set of management tools that cut across all the functional areas of business—from strategy to human resources to finance, accounting, and operations. They draw on the interdisciplinary research of the Michigan faculty. Yet each book is written so a serious manager can read it quickly and act immediately. I think you will find that they are books that will make a significant difference to you and your organization.

Robert E. Quinn, Consulting Editor
M.E. Tracy Distinguished Professor
University of Michigan Business School

Preface

During my career as a professor at the University of Michigan Business School, I have directed and taught in degree and executive programs offered at the University of Michigan and at other locations in Europe, Asia, and South America. These programs have enabled me to work with colleagues who are leaders in their fields, such as C.K. Prahalad in corporate strategy and David Ulrich in human resources, and with managers from the world's leading corporations.

I have also had the opportunity to serve in a managerial role as associate dean in charge of the University of Michigan Executive Education Center, which has been recognized by the business press as the leading provider of executive education in the world. In this role, I worked with senior executives from global corporations and consulting firms in designing customized programs for their managers. During my service as associate dean, the Executive Education Center expanded internationally by establishing offices in Europe and Asia.

These two experiences—working with talented colleagues and managers from around the world and heading a large international center devoted to executive education—have led to three insights regarding the relationship between law and business. First, business law is rapidly changing in response to the globalization of business. For example, there has been significant convergence of the law of various countries relating to contracts, environmental protection, and securities regulation.

Second, managers have an increasing appreciation for the importance of law. For example, an analysis of program evaluations completed by over nine hundred senior managers attending University of Michigan executive programs revealed that law is one of three most important subjects (along with finance and human resources) among business school required courses. The reason is obvious: law touches almost every aspect of a manager's work.

Third, the combination of legal change and the ubiquity of law just noted has created new opportunities for competitive advantage. Specifically, savvy managers can use the law to reduce their costs and develop products that are unique or priced lower than those of competitors. But to achieve competitive advantage, these managers need a plan.

This book provides the plan, a four-step process called the Manager's Legal Plan, which is designed for managers who have responsibility for their companies' success. The plan described in this book is also useful to business school students whose goal is to attain a business leadership position, to corporate attorneys who work with managers in the pursuit of competitive advantage, and to law students who plan to specialize in business law.

The four steps of the Manager's Legal Plan enable managers to use law for competitive advantage as they address legal concerns on a daily basis. The steps are

1. Understand the law.
2. React to legal problems through flight or fight.
3. Develop business strategies and solutions to prevent legal problems.

4. Climb to the balcony to reframe legal concerns as business concerns.

The Manager's Legal Plan and its rationale are explained in Chapter One. Chapters Two through Four illustrate how the process can be used to address several of the most vexing problems facing managers today: product liability, workers' compensation, wrongful discharge, sexual harassment, and environmental regulation. The book concludes in Chapter Five with a review of three topics that apply to a wide range of legal concerns: obtaining and using the best legal resources, resolving disputes in a cost-effective manner, and using the Manager's Legal Plan to encourage ethical decision making.

■ Acknowledgments

I want to acknowledge and thank Bob Quinn, the M.E. Tracy Distinguished Professor at the University of Michigan Business School, for conceiving and developing the UMBS Management Series. Thanks also to the Jossey-Bass team for the professional support that led to the publication of this book. Through this project, I have had the privilege of working with Alan Venable, one of the best developmental editors in the country. Other team members who played an important role in the completion of the book are Cedric Crocker, Kathe Sweeney, Cheryl Greenway, Rachel Anderson, and Sheri Gilbert.
    I owe a special debt of gratitude to the managers with whom I have worked in the United States, Europe, Asia, and South America. The Manager's Legal Plan is the result of their advice and encouragement. This book reflects their success in achieving competitive advantage for their companies.

January 2002   George J. Siedel
                                                  Ann Arbor, Michigan

Seizing Competitive Advantage

A Legal Plan for Managers

ongratulations! Last year the chief executive officer of your company named you general manager of one of the firm's most important divisions. Your first year as head of the division has been a success, as you have exceeded the goals set by corporate headquarters.

Condolences! You have no time to savor your early success. You and the CEO recently analyzed business trends. You both anticipate that the market for your products will become much more competitive, especially with a recent increase in foreign competition. The CEO emphasizes that your division must gain competitive advantage over rival companies in order to survive.

Beyond concerns about the survival of your division, you have other worries. If you fail as leader of the division, it will be difficult to return to a lower-level position—and in the current economic climate you may be unable to find a general manager position at another company. You also feel responsible for the division's employees. The division is the largest employer in your town, and a shutdown would devastate the local economy, as well as the families of your employees.

As you plan for the coming year, you develop a list of your goals. High on your list are attracting, developing, and retaining the best employees, thinking and planning more strategically about the future, maintaining a high-performance climate in your division, and improving the satisfaction of your customers. To this list you add a personal goal—managing time and stress—because your work increasingly pulls you away from your family and you have little time for recreation.

You then list three key legal obstacles that might prevent you from achieving your goals (while also increasing your stress levels). These problems are increased workers' compensation costs, high product liability insurance premiums, and major costs incurred in complying with environmental regulations.

Beyond these general concerns, you are worried about a lawsuit that might have a significant impact on the company and on you personally. A year ago, when you took over leadership of the division, you fired an employee who was not performing to your expectations. The employee has now sued you and the company, claiming breach of contract. The employee also claims that you defamed him by making untrue statements about his performance. As a result of this lawsuit, you are reluctant to terminate other poor performers, for fear that they might also file suit. Therefore, you write down a fourth problem—the wrongful termination lawsuit. Your goals and obstacles are listed in Exhibit 1.1.

Exhibit 1.1. Your Planning List.

Goals

1. Attract, develop, retain best employees.
2. Think and plan strategically about future.
3. Maintain a high performance climate.
4. Improve customer satisfaction.
5. Manage time and stress.

Problems

1. Increased workers' compensation costs.
2. Product liability insurance premiums.
3. Compliance with environmental regulations.
4. Wrongful termination lawsuit.

If it is any consolation—and misery does indeed love company—you have lots of company among managers at firms around the world. Achieving competitive advantage is critical to the success and even the survival of companies that cross a variety of industries and cultures. Managers at these companies share the goals listed in Exhibit 1.1. In a study based on over seventeen hundred responses from entry-level, middle, and senior managers, researchers at the University of Michigan Business School concluded that the goals on this list match the leading challenges faced by managers worldwide.[1]

The legal problems on your list, such as environmental and workers' compensation costs, also rank among the top business concerns.[2] Legal issues in general have emerged as the most important factor in the external environment in which business operates. It is estimated that Fortune 500 executives spend 20 percent of their time on litigation-related matters.[3] It is no wonder that business executives attending management development programs rank law among the three most important business topics, along with human resources and finance.[4]

John Seeley Brown, director of Xerox Research Center, once observed that "Managers don't make products; they make sense."[5]

In your leadership role, as you attempt to make sense of the legal challenges in your competitive environment, it is easy to become mesmerized by the complexity of the law, like a deer in the lights of oncoming highway traffic. In a sense, the goal of this book is to provide a plan—the Manager's Legal Plan—that will enable you to cross the legal highways that intersect your business strategies while minimizing the risk of being struck down by legal liability. In a broader sense, however, the goal is to help you recognize that the so-called legal problems on your list are in reality opportunities for competitive advantage.

This chapter will introduce the Manager's Legal Plan by first explaining the business concept of competitive advantage. The chapter will next describe the traditional approach used by managers when confronted with legal problems. The traditional approach will then be contrasted with a different approach that enables you to use the law to achieve competitive advantage. The chapter will close with a brief overview of the remaining chapters in the book.

■ The Essence of Competitive Advantage

The concept of competitive advantage is central to business success around the world. Because this concept is subject to differing interpretations, it is useful at the outset to provide a working definition as a point of reference for the chapters that follow.

The definition of competitive advantage is straightforward: Your goal in business is to gain an *advantage* over your *competitors*. If you were a college basketball coach, you would try to gain advantage over competitors by recruiting athletes who are taller and faster than players on opposing teams. You would attempt to develop game plans that maximize your strengths and exploit your opponents' weaknesses. You would develop a training program and organize practices to improve the performance of your athletes. In other words, your goals as a coach would be similar to the business goals in Exhibit 1.1.

Of course, college basketball teams and businesses use different measures of success. In college basketball, the success of a coach is determined primarily by whether fans are satisfied with the number of games that the team wins during the season. In business, a manager must also satisfy the fans (customers) but must do so in a manner that produces profits for the firm's owners.

As a result, a company seeking competitive advantage must satisfy two requirements. First, the company must create value for its customers that is superior to the value offered by its competitors. Superior value, as Harvard professor Michael Porter explains in his book *Competitive Advantage*, "stems from offering lower prices than competitors for equivalent benefits or providing unique benefits that more than offset a higher price."[6] Second, the amount that buyers are willing to pay for this value must exceed the company's costs if the firm is to be profitable. As Porter puts it, "Competitive advantage grows fundamentally out of value a firm is able to create for its buyers that exceeds the firm's cost of creating it."[7]

As we will see in the chapters that follow, law plays an important role in both reducing costs and creating value for your customers—by enabling you to offer either lower prices or products that provide unique benefits. If all companies took full advantage of their legal resources, any resulting advantage over the competition would disappear. However, because law is an untapped source of competitive advantage that will continue to be misunderstood by many managers, selected companies should be able to leverage their legal resources into a source of competitive advantage that is sustainable over the long term.

■ The Conventional Approach to Legal Problems

The approach most managers use when dealing with legal matters contains many pitfalls. Managers often start with a mindset that separates legal issues from the strategic and operational concerns of the business. As Exhibit 1.1 implies, too often, legal concerns are treated as problems to be resolved as quickly as possible so that attention can be focused on business goals. This attitude overlooks the fundamental point that, even if legal matters are viewed as problems, they affect the business goals of both you and your competitors. The companies that can best resolve these problems—and the managers who develop bridges between the lists in Exhibit 1.1—create an opportunity to seize competitive advantage. In other words, successful managers ask the question: How can this legal problem create an opportunity to gain an advantage over our competitors?

Given the current approach that too often separates legal and business concerns, managers typically engage in a two-step process when addressing legal concerns. The first step is to meet with an attorney to discuss their rights and obligations. For instance, in responding to the wrongful termination case filed by your former employee, you would first meet with your attorney to determine whether the claim has any merit. During the course of your conversation, the attorney would explain the breach of contract and defamation claims, and would also discuss whether it is likely that the employee would win in court, the potential damages, and the costs of the litigation.

Following the briefing by an attorney, the second step is to activate the flight-or-fight responses that have developed in humans over millions of years and allow us to survive in dangerous situations. In a legal sense, there are two flight options for your company (see Figure 1.1). First, flight might involve settlement of a specific case, such as your wrongful termination law-

	Specific Cases	Broader Concerns
Flight	Settle	Move Business
Fight	Litigate	Law Reform

Figure 1.1. Conventional Approaches to Legal Problems.

suit. Second, if certain types of cases are so common that they prevent your company from achieving competitive advantage, then flight might involve movement of the business to another state or country. Examples include situations where your state workers' compensation costs might cause you to move your factory to another state, or federal environmental burdens might cause you to move operations to another country.

The fight response also includes two options. One option is to fight individual claims in court on a case-by-case basis. The other option is to take the fight to a higher level and fight to reform laws that have a detrimental impact on business. For instance, in addition to fighting individual workers' compensation cases, your company might push for legal reform that would reduce the financial burden of workers' compensation.

For reasons stated in the sections that follow, the traditional flight-or-fight responses have become more difficult—or in some situations impossible—to execute successfully. Thus, in a global economy, the manager's conventional approach to legal concerns is often no longer realistic.

Difficulties with the Flight Response

Both of the characteristic flight responses can lead to problems in the current environment. Sometimes, neither settlement of a specific case nor movement of your business makes sense.

The Strategy of Settling Specific Cases

Flight from litigation through settlement of a specific case often appears to be a logical course of action—even when it is likely that your company will win if the case goes to trial. If you can settle a case for $50,000 and it will cost you $100,000 to litigate the case even if you win, common sense tells you to settle.

However, the total cost of settlement might be much higher than litigation costs when, by settling the case, you signal to plaintiffs and their attorneys that you are willing to pay to set-tle future cases to avoid a trial even when you have a winning case. Professor John Coffee of Columbia Law School, in com-menting on a 2001 Merrill Lynch settlement with a client who lost money on a stock market investment, put it this way: "[Set-tlement] is like putting out warm milk for a stray cat that meows. You get 30 more cats the next night. This will create an incentive for others" to sue.[8] Settlements also result in additional costs that far exceed the amount of the payments. For instance, as discussed in Chapter Three, the costs of workers' compensa-tion—including lost productivity and expenses incurred in train-ing replacements—far exceed amounts paid in settlements with workers.

Flight through settlement can also be problematic when there are two defendants. A settlement offer made by a plaintiff to the two defendants—for instance, in a lawsuit filed by a con-sumer against your company and another company—can create a problem called the prisoner's dilemma. For example, two hy-pothetical prisoners, Bonnie and Clyde, have been charged with bank robbery and assault. A police detective interrogates them in separate rooms. Bonnie and Clyde know that even if they don't confess to the charges, the police have enough evidence to convict them for assault, which carries a prison term of three years. The police tell them that if only one of them confesses, that person will receive a prison term of one year and the other will receive an eight-year term. If both confess, the prison term for both charges would be four years each. The police do not allow Bonnie and Clyde to communicate with each other. If you were Bonnie, would you confess?

As Figure 1.2 illustrates, it appears that the most rational strategy is for Bonnie (and Clyde) to confess. That is, no matter what choice Clyde makes (confess or do not confess), Bonnie's best strategy is to confess. The dilemma for these prisoners is that, although it is rational for each of them as an individual to confess, collectively they end up in a worse position (four-year prison terms) than if they had both refused to confess (in which case they would receive three-year terms).[9]

If, instead of prisoners, Bonnie and Clyde are two small competing companies (Bonnie, Inc. and Clyde, Inc.) that make components for a toy, a similar dilemma may arise. For instance,

	Clyde	
	Don't Confess	Confess
Bonnie Don't Confess	Bonnie — 3 years Clyde — 3 years	Bonnie — 8 years Clyde — 1 years
Confess	Bonnie — 1 years Clyde — 8 years	Bonnie — 4 years Clyde — 4 years

Figure 1.2. Prisoner's Dilemma.

a child sustains minor injuries while using the toy and an attorney files a $300,000 lawsuit against both companies. The case has little merit and the attorney hopes to extract a settlement from the companies rather than going to trial. The two companies have filed claims against each other, arguing that if there is any liability, it should fall on the other company.

If both companies refuse to settle, they will each incur litigation costs of $30,000 in asking for a dismissal of the case (which they are certain a court would grant). The plaintiff's attorney offers each company the opportunity to settle immediately, promising to accept a settlement of $10,000 from one defendant if that defendant agrees to help in the case against the remaining defendant. (In one version of this type of settlement, named a "Mary Carter" agreement after a case involving the Mary Carter Paint Company,[10] the plaintiff settles with one defendant for a certain amount. This amount is then reduced depending on how much the other defendant eventually has to pay the plaintiff.) Given the settling defendant's assistance to the plaintiff, the other defendant would be unable to obtain an early dismissal, but would still probably win at trial—at a cost of $80,000 in legal expenses. The plaintiff's attorney is willing to settle immediately with both companies for $40,000 each.

If you manage Bonnie, Inc., it appears that your most rational strategy—similar to the decision made by prisoner Bonnie— is to settle (as illustrated in Figure 1.3). But you face the same dilemma as the prisoners in that, although it is rational for each company to settle, they are both in a worse position (each settling for $40,000) than if they had refused to settle (in which case their costs would have been $30,000 each). But because they are competitors and adversaries in the litigation, they are unlikely to cooperate. Even if they did reach a tentative agreement, each company is afraid that the other might back out at the last minute or might enter into a secret Mary Carter agreement.

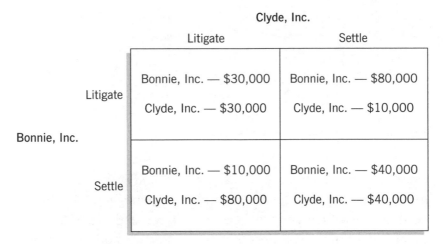

Figure 1.3. Company Settlement Dilemma.

Thus flight from litigation through settlement is problematic. There is a risk that single-party decisions to settle based on a simple cost-benefit analysis (it may be cheaper to settle than to litigate a winning case) and decisions in the two-party prisoner's dilemma scenario fuel litigation by encouraging attorneys to file lawsuits even when their chance of success at trial is slight.

The Strategy of Moving the Company
When certain types of liability, such as workers' compensation payments or environmental costs, become burdensome, it is tempting to consider the flight option of moving your business to another state or country. Under traditional notions of *comparative* advantage, certain countries have a comparative advantage over others as a result of cost advantages, including legal costs. But in a global economy, countries face difficulty in achieving comparative legal advantage for two reasons illustrated by Figure 1.4: the cross-border movement of goods, services, and investments, and the increasing convergence of legal rules and regulations.

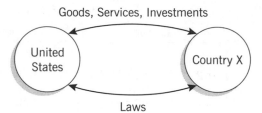

Figure 1.4. Decline of Comparative Advantage.

Cross-Border Movement of Goods, Services, and Investments. The movement of goods, services, and investments across political borders means that you will be subject to regulation and liability in other countries regardless of where the goods and services are produced. For example, if you are operating a plant in Country X (see Figure 1.4), you are subject to liability for injuries caused by your goods in the United States.

The rationale for this liability was explained in a 1988 Nevada case involving the band Judas Priest. One evening two young men went to an empty churchyard and attempted to commit suicide. The first man succeeded, after propping a sawed-off shotgun under his chin and pulling the trigger. The second man somehow survived a similar suicide attempt, but suffered severe injuries. The survivor and the mother of the decedent filed a lawsuit in Nevada against the members of Judas Priest, who were residents of Great Britain. The plaintiffs claimed that the suicidal actions were caused by one of the band's albums, called "Stained Class."

Before deciding whether the band was liable, the Nevada court first had to determine whether it had the right to hear a case involving residents of another country. The court determined that the courts of Nevada could hear cases like this because "the band members consciously and deliberately chose to develop a world-wide market."[11]

In today's global economy, especially as electronic commerce facilitates global product reach, companies increasingly choose "to develop a world-wide market." As a result, they must be prepared to defend lawsuits in other countries, even those that they eventually win—as did the members of Judas Priest. In other words, in a world where the mantra "think globally, act locally" applies to law as well as to other aspects of business, the traditional option of flight to a country with minimal legal requirements has been considerably diluted.

Convergence of Legal Rules. Laws increasingly move across political borders, resulting in convergence of the legal rules that govern business practice. In many cases, this convergence takes place through the spread of U.S. rules and regulations to other countries. An article in the *Economist* on a new California law begins by describing this familiar legal migration pattern: "California today, America tomorrow—and the rest of the world the day after."[12] However, Figure 1.4 illustrates that law reform moves in two directions, as laws in other countries also influence legal developments in the United States.

Law can be divided into two broad categories—substantive and procedural—both of which have been affected by convergence in recent years. *Substantive law* deals with the substance of the law—the legal rules and regulations that govern business operations and management decision making. *Procedural law* is the body of law relating to the enforcement of substantive law.

The following examples illustrate the convergence of substantive law.

- *Contract law.* A relatively new international law, the United Nations Convention on Contracts for the International Sale of Goods, establishes a uniform set of rules for contracts involving buyers and sellers from different countries. Originally ratified by the United States and ten other countries in 1988, these rules now have been adopted by close to sixty countries. By reducing legal differences from one country to another, the Convention lowers contract law barriers to international trade.

- *Product liability.* Product liability, your company's liability for defective products, will be discussed in Chapter Two. As noted in that chapter, U.S.-style product liability has spread to the European Union and to the Pacific Rim, including Australia, China, the Philippines, and Japan. Describing product liability laws in Europe in an article titled "Sue Everywhere," *Forbes* magazine notes that "savvy companies are starting to realize they face a whole new continent of potential plaintiffs."[13]

- *Environmental law.* Here, too, U.S.-style liability has spread throughout the world. As the head of environmental affairs for a multinational company confided to me, based on his analysis of environmental regulations in countries around the world, "it seems as though other countries have adopted carbon copies of American law." Environmental regulation will be explored further in Chapter Four.

- *Securities regulation.* Countries around the world have come to realize that fair and consistent regulation is necessary if investors are to have faith in the securities market. For example, many countries in recent years have adopted insider-trading laws that are similar to U.S. law.

- *Sexual harassment.* Laws that originated in the United States relating to sexual harassment have now become the international standard. Sexual harassment will be covered in Chapter Three.

- *Anti-bribery law.* The United States led the fight against bribery with the adoption of the Foreign Corrupt Practices Act in 1977. Because other leading industrial countries did not have similar laws, U.S. companies claimed that foreign firms had an unfair advantage. For instance, it is estimated that in one year alone, bribes for competitors caused U.S. companies to lose over $15 billion.[14] But in 1997, over two dozen countries signed an anti-bribery agreement that has leveled the playing field for U.S. companies.

Even U.S.-style law that has not officially been adopted by other countries often has an extraterritorial reach. For example, U.S. employees working for U.S. firms are protected by U.S. employment laws when working in other countries. Other laws, such as antitrust law, apply to non-Americans acting outside the United States when their conduct has an impact on the United States. And U.S. law is frequently embedded in codes of conduct adopted by multinational companies. In total, according to international lawyer Gregory J. Wallance, "The cold war paradigm was the United States as global policeman. The post-cold-war paradigm is the United States as global attorney."[15]

Procedural law, as noted earlier, deals with the enforcement of substantive law. Historically, six features of the legal process distinguished the United States from the rest of the world. In recent years convergence has had an impact on these features in two ways. First, the impact of some features (see the first three items on the following list) has been diminished by law reform in the United States. Second, other features (the second half of the list) are being exported to other countries.

- *Jury trials.* Unlike most countries in the world, the United States still allows litigants the option of a jury trial in civil lawsuits. However, the right to jury trial has diminished recently as a result of a combination of factors, including an increase in the use of arbitration, laws in most states that limit the amount of damages that juries can award, requirements that judges hear certain types of cases, and dismissal of cases by judges before they reach a jury. In the words of Ron Cohen, the chair of the American Bar Association Litigation Section: "For the first time in our country's history, the future of the jury system is in serious jeopardy."[16]

- *Punitive damages.* The United States is unusual in allowing plaintiffs to recover punitive damages when defendants have engaged in egregious behavior. Over the past several years, however, many states have enacted legislation limiting punitive damages.

- *Legal expenses.* Unlike other countries, which typically use a "loser pays" approach, in the United States the winning party must pay most of its own legal costs. This traditional American rule is being eroded as new legislation in the United States frequently provides that the loser must pay the winner's full legal costs.

- *Contingency fees.* In the United States, contingency fee agreements—where the payment to a lawyer is contingent on the outcome of the case—are legal. For example, if you agree to pay your attorney a 30 percent contingency fee and the jury awards you $10 million, the lawyer's fee is $3 million. If the jury decides that you are not entitled to damages, the attorney receives 30 percent of 0. Other countries have joined the United States in allowing contingency fees, including Canada, the United Kingdom, Japan, and China.

- *Discovery.* Discovery is the process used by attorneys to locate evidence and witnesses for use at trial. For instance, the opposing lawyer has the right to search through your business records for evidence that might be relevant to the case. E-mail has been an especially fruitful source of evidence. In one case, after Atlantic Richfield (ARCO) sold its solar energy subsidiary to Siemens, ARCO employee e-mail messages such as the following were discovered: "We will attempt to finesse past Siemens the fact that we have had a great amount of trouble in successfully transitioning technology from the laboratory to the manufacturing floor." These e-mail messages contributed to a Siemens lawsuit requesting $146 million in damages.[17] In recent years, other countries have moved closer to U.S.-style discovery. In

Japan, for example, rules adopted in 1998 make it easier to obtain evidence from the opposing side.

- *Class actions.* If your company illegally overcharges me $10 for your product, it is unlikely that I will bother filing suit for this small amount of damages. But if the company overcharges a million customers, a lawsuit filed on behalf of these customers—called a class action—converts a $10 claim to a $10 million lawsuit (or possibly $30 million if damages are trebled, as they might be in this type of case). Critics of class actions claim that the real winners in class actions are attorneys, whose 30 percent contingency fee would net them millions of dollars. Their clients, on the other hand, would receive the price of lunch (70 percent of $10, or of $30 as a best case) *before* expenses were taken out of their share. Despite their controversial nature, class actions are now allowed in a number of other countries, including Australia, Canada, the United Kingdom, China, and Japan.

We have examined several examples of the convergence of substantive and procedural law. It is said that a butterfly flapping its wings in the United States can cause a typhoon in Asia. Similar to this "butterfly effect," convergence of the law causes a legal development in one country to change business practice elsewhere. Several years ago, for instance, McDonald's was sued in the United States in a controversial case involving an elderly woman who was burned when she spilled her cup of McDonald's coffee. The woman was awarded close to $3 million, although she later settled the case for substantially less. After this case was resolved, I traveled to Argentina to address the national association of corporate lawyers. While in Buenos Aires, I visited a local McDonald's and purchased a cup of coffee. Printed in four places on the small cup in bright red letters were warnings that the coffee was hot: "PRECAUCION: CALIENTE!" These warnings were no doubt prompted by a legal decision in a country that, while far away in a geographic sense, has become much closer legally to the rest of the world.

Difficulties with the Fight Response

Flight from legal concerns—through settlement of specific cases or movement of business operations to a supposedly friendlier legal environment—is often unrealistic in a global economy. The other option engrained into our genetic code is to stand and fight. There are two legal contexts for legal battles, each representing a different form of government regulation of business: specific cases in which court decisions represent a form of business regulation and larger legislative and regulatory arenas in which law reform battles are fought.

The option of fighting specific cases has already been covered, in the course of discussing the settlement of cases. That discussion noted problems with litigating individual cases. In cases where your company is a sole defendant, litigation costs are substantial even when you are confident that you would win at trial. And cases with two defendants can create a prisoner's dilemma scenario, in which a decision to litigate may be irrational, at least when the defendants do not communicate with each other. A decision by both defendants to litigate also makes it easier for a plaintiff's attorney to prove that they were at fault. In their attacks on each other, the defendants prove the plaintiff's case, leaving only the question of which of them should bear all or most of the liability. For example, to the plaintiffs' delight, defendants Ford and Firestone are pitted against each other in hundreds of personal injury lawsuits filed against them for injuries resulting from the use of Ford sport-utility vehicles equipped with Firestone tires.

This section will concentrate on the larger arenas in which the battle for law reform takes place. At first glance, law reform would seem to offer an opportunity to secure competitive advantage by lowering a company's legal costs. However, just as two-defendant litigation might produce a prisoner's dilemma, law reform creates another form of dilemma called the public goods dilemma. The dilemma is that the outcome of law reform—say, a change in workers' compensation law that reduces company payments considerably—is a public good. As such, the new law benefits all companies, whether or not they invested their time and money in the reform effort. As professor Leigh Thompson of Northwestern University bluntly notes: "Those who fail to contribute are known as defectors or free riders. Those who pay while others free ride are affectionately known as suckers."[18]

Even when all companies in a particular industry contribute equally to law reform that benefits only their industry (in other words, when there are initially no free riders), the reform might provide little or no competitive advantage to your company. For instance, a reduction in workers' compensation payments might make the industry as a whole more profitable, but companies will not share equally in these profits. The lion's share of the profits will go to the companies that, as Porter puts it, create superior value for their customers by offering lower prices or unique benefits while keeping costs down. And the increased profitability of the industry may well attract new competition, free riders from the outside.

Efforts to improve the legal system are often noble and necessary to improve the national economy. Before your company invests resources in reform initiatives, however, you should carefully analyze the goal of law reform. If your goal is to serve a higher purpose, such as benefiting society, then your efforts might be justified. But if your goal is to increase your own competitive advantage, you should carefully answer the question: "What's in it for my company?"

In some cases a change in the law may provide your company with direct competitive advantage. For instance, time limits protecting intellectual property are sometimes extended in a way that protects specific products. In 1998, the life of copyrighted works was extended from seventy-five to ninety-five years, a change supported by Disney Corporation to protect its exclusive rights to Donald Duck and Mickey Mouse. Suddenly Disney competitors were playing on a different field. In the words of Wharton professor G. Richard Shell: "There has been a lot of legislative maneuvering to gain competitive advantage. To use a football analogy, it's like making first and goal and suddenly finding they have lengthened the field by 30 yards."[19] But in other situations, where there are no specific benefits, it is easy for companies to become so enthusiastic about a cause that they overlook the fact that the benefits do not provide competitive advantage.

Thus all four conventional approaches to legal problems depicted in Figure 1.1 are flawed:

- Settling specific cases can encourage future litigation or invoke the prisoner's dilemma.
- Moving your company is often unhelpful, given the global convergence of law.
- Fighting specific cases is often not cost-effective.
- Investing in law reform might benefit your industry or the country in general without creating competitive advantage for your company.

■ The Manager's Legal Plan

The picture that emerges from a review of the conventional flight-or-fight approach to legal problems is common throughout the business world. Managers faced with myriad business concerns frequently take a reactive approach to legal problems. In this reactive posture, the traditional flight-or-fight responses are often unsatisfactory, for the reasons just described. Given their reactive stance, it is not surprising that managers often view law as an obstacle and that they tend to mentally separate legal concerns from the issues that are considered more central to competitive advantage.

A problem that underlies this managerial mindset toward the law is that managers often feel incapable of creating a plan for dealing with legal matters. But a plan does not have to be great or perfect; even a faulty plan can be better than nothing. Albert Szent-Gyorti, Nobel Laureate in medicine, tells the story of a military reconnaissance team that was lost in the Swiss Alps following a snowstorm. The soldiers had given up hope of returning to their main unit alive when one of them discovered a map in their equipment. Having the map calmed the soldiers and, with the sense of direction provided by the map, they found their main unit. Upon their return, they showed the map to their lieutenant, who discovered that it was a map of the Pyrenees, rather than the Alps.[20]

This story illustrates that a leader does not need a perfect legal or strategic plan to calm employees and get them moving in the right direction. When a manager is faced with a confusing situation, be it a rapidly changing legal environment or new forms of competition, simply having a plan is often enough to inspire action that can lead to positive results. As noted by Karl Weick, my colleague at the University of Michigan Business School and one of the world's leading organizational theorists: "Followers are often lost and even the leader is not sure where to go. All the leaders know is that the plan or the map they have in front of them are not sufficient to get them out. What the leader has to do, when faced with this situation, is instill some confidence in people, get them moving in some general direction, and be sure they look closely at cues created by their actions so that they learn where they were and get some better idea of where they are and where they want to be."[21]

Taking action, any action, is often better than the paralysis and confusion that can result when managers encounter legal problems. In this spirit, the following four-step Manager's Legal Plan is intended to enable managers to move from a reactive approach toward legal concerns to an ability to actively use the law to uncover and develop new forms of competitive advantage.

The first two steps of the plan build on the conventional approach that managers currently use in addressing legal concerns; the third step represents best practices of leading companies; the last step goes further.

Step One: Understand the Law

The conventional first step in addressing a legal problem is to meet with your attorney to discuss your legal rights and obligations, as you would do in handling your wrongful termination lawsuit. Step One in the Manager's Legal Plan is similar, except that the scope of the conversation goes beyond the specific litigation to a broader understanding of the law. You should, for instance, ask your attorney to provide a broader perspective on wrongful discharge lawsuits. What are they? What theories do plaintiffs assert in general (even though they are not all raised in your lawsuit)? What types of liability are associated with these lawsuits? And so on.

As discussed in later chapters, an obvious reason for this broader legal briefing is to prevent future litigation. Beyond this goal the broader briefing is essential to your career growth. As you move higher in the organization you will increasingly face business decisions that have legal implications. You will also discuss legal matters with a variety of parties, including customers, suppliers, employees, government officials, the media, shareholders, the board of directors, and creditors. According to Ben Heineman, senior vice president of General Electric, "People who lead corporations need to have an appreciation for the whole public side of their job as they go higher and higher up the ladder. Law [is] a significant part of any corporate entity's life."[22] A former CEO of General Motors reputedly put it more bluntly: "My lawyer and I go steady."

Because managers need to understand the law, one of your most important resources is an attorney who has the ability to teach. A survey of CEOs by the American Corporate Counsel Association concluded that the most important role of a corporate attorney is that of an educator on legal issues.[23] The study of business law is also an important facet of a manager's formal education. In the United States, the legal environment of business is a key component of undergraduate, MBA, and executive education. Outside the United States, the importance of understanding business law is highlighted by the fact that a major in law is a popular alternative to a business major for students who intend to become managers.

Step Two: React to Legal Problems Through Flight or Fight

The second step is much like the conventional approach to legal problems. That is, your flight-or-fight mechanism will trigger an attempt to use one of the solutions summarized in Figure 1.1. While resort to one of these solutions is often inevitable, you should keep in mind their limitations in the global economy, as described earlier in this chapter.

Step Three: Develop Business Strategies and Solutions to Prevent Legal Problems

The third step in the Manager's Legal Plan goes beyond the traditional approaches by searching for business strategies and solutions to legal problems, rather than flight-or-fight solutions. While this sounds like a logical next step, especially when the flight-or-fight response fails, managers commonly forget to apply sound business judgment when faced with legal decisions. I have observed this phenomenon in a legal decision-making exercise that I have used in my work with hundreds of experienced managers and MBA students. When faced with a litigation decision, these executives and students become so focused on the legal issues that they forget to use a financial analysis that includes calculation of net present value and opportunity costs. As a result they frequently decide to continue litigation that, from a business perspective, should be settled.

But Step Three goes beyond applying business tools to litigation. For example, a manager confronted with wrongful discharge litigation would take action that moves beyond the narrow decision to settle or fight. As discussed in greater detail in Chapter Three, the company's hiring practices should be reviewed, company documents should be revised, and employees should receive training that will prevent them from making statements that could result in liability.

Step Four: Climb to the Balcony— Reframe Legal Concerns as Business Concerns

It is tempting to conclude the Manager's Legal Plan at Step Three. After all, once you have completed the three steps, you have a broad understanding of the legal problem, you have exhausted flight-or-fight options, and you have applied best business practices in an attempt to resolve the problem.

However one remaining question has been overlooked: Is your problem solely legal in nature? In other words, are you framing the problem correctly? Mental frames that help us simplify and organize the complexity in our world are necessary for rational decision making. But simplification often comes at a cost. In viewing the world through a particular window, such as the window provided by a legal problem, we see only part of the landscape. In narrowing the scope of our vision, we risk what decision researchers call frame blindness, which is similar to the blind spot in a car's rearview mirror. By failing to take into account the entire picture when making decisions, we often over-look the best options.[24]

Your challenge as a manager, when dealing with a problem that appears to relate narrowly to a particular function—whether law or marketing or finance or manufacturing—is to step back from the details of the problem and attempt to broaden the frame. This book will provide numerous examples of the art of reframing "legal problems" as business opportunities. In his book *Getting Past No,* author William Ury uses the phrase "going to the balcony" as a metaphor for the mental detachment that is necessary when you are attacked or rebuffed by the other side during a negotiation.[25] In your role as a manager, a trip to the balcony can give you a broader perspective of the entire playing field without the blind spots that hinder your decision making when you are closer to the action. This broader perspective may enable you to reframe what you originally thought was a legal problem as a business opportunity. This, in turn, will allow you to generate new options for gaining competitive advantage. Though you may be unable to reframe every legal problem that you face, the attempt should at least encourage you and others in your organization to think about where you are and where you want to be—much like the map of the Pyrenees that saved the reconnaissance team lost in the Alps.

■ How This Book Is Organized

The chapters that follow will apply the four steps of the Manager's Legal Plan to legal issues that relate to various stakeholder groups—parties with an interest in your company. In creating value for the owners of your company, the shareholders, you must manage relationships with a variety of other stakeholders in a cost-effective manner. Especially important among them are your customers, your employees, and society at large, represented by government. The Manager's Legal Plan will be used to explore the most controversial legal problems relating to these stakeholders. Chapter Two will focus on customers' product liability lawsuits, as well as hidden new product opportunities represented by this type of litigation. Chapter Three will address several legal matters relating to employees—workers' compensation, wrongful discharge, and sexual harassment—and how the changing nature of the employment relationship might produce opportunities for retaining the talent that is essential for business success. Chapter Four will show that even government regulation as stringent as environmental regulation can create opportunities for competitive advantage. Since specific legal plans will vary across companies and industries, the goal in each of these chapters is not to provide a definitive list of solutions. But these chapters will offer concrete examples of ways in which the Manager's Legal Plan can generate opportunities for competitive advantage.

Beyond the controversial issues covered in Chapters Two through Four that relate to key company stakeholder groups, several generic legal matters apply to a wide variety of legal concerns. For instance, given the importance of the law to business success, how can you ensure that you have the best legal resources and that you are maximizing the value of your legal talent? What tools are available for you to resolve disputes and how can you use systems design to best apply these tools? And how can your use of the law to achieve competitive advantage encourage ethical decision making within your company? These questions will be addressed in Chapter Five.

CHAPTER SUMMARY

Law plays an important role in achieving competitive advantage, as it enables companies to achieve cost reduction and develop products that are either unique or priced lower than those of competitors. However, conventional "flight-or-fight" approaches to legal problems do not allow managers to make best use of the law to gain competitive advantage. For example:

1. Settling cases might encourage future litigation. Additional problems, in the form of the prisoner's dilemma, arise when a company has a co-defendant.
2. Moving the company to a friendlier legal environment does not work in a global economy for two reasons. First, as a result of the cross-border movement of goods, services, and investments, companies are increasingly subject to legal rules and regulations beyond their home country. Second, convergence of legal rules has become more common. Substantive law has converged in the areas of contract law, product liability, environmental law, securities regulation, sexual harassment, and anti-bribery law. Convergence has even occurred in areas relating to the legal process that once distinguished the United States from the rest of the world: jury trials, punitive damages, legal expenses, contingency fees, discovery, and class actions.
3. Fighting individual cases often does not make economic sense when they can be settled for less than the cost of litigation.
4. Fighting for law reform also may not make economic sense absent the potential for competitive advantage. As a result of the public goods dilemma, for instance, a company's investment in law reform might benefit free riders.

Given drawbacks with conventional approaches to legal problems, a new approach is necessary to maximize the use of law to gain competitive advantage. This new approach, called the Manager's Legal Plan, involves the following four-step process:

Step One. Understand the law in a broad sense, rather than just the specific issues you face when addressing a legal concern.
Step Two. Determine whether the conventional "flight-or-fight" approaches listed in Figure 1.1 can be used to resolve your legal problem.

Step Three. Develop business strategies and solutions to minimize future legal problems.

Step Four. Reframe legal concerns as business opportunities.

The chapters that follow will provide specific examples of how this plan can be used to achieve competitive advantage.

Questions to Consider

1. When you introduce a new product, do you think globally about the law and the impact of rules and regulations in countries where the product will be marketed?
2. When your company invests in law reform, do you consider the public goods dilemma and the advantages that the reform will provide to your company, as opposed to the industry in general?
3. Do you have a plan for using the law to achieve competitive advantage?
4. After a legal problem has been resolved, do you use your experience to prevent recurrence of the problem?
5. Do you ask your attorneys to provide you with a broader perspective on the legal matters that require your decision?
6. Do you attempt to reframe legal problems as business opportunities?

Meet Your Customer Needs

Moving from Product Liability to Product Innovation

Chapter One explored the increasing importance of law in a global economy. The chapter also described a four step process, the Manager's Legal Plan, that enables you to use the law to seize competitive advantage for your company. This and the next two chapters apply this process to several critically important business issues: product liability, workers' compensation, wrongful discharge, sexual harassment, and environmental regulation. Each of these issues affects important stakeholders in your company. Product liability principally affects customers; workers' compensation, wrongful discharge, and sexual harassment primarily affect employees; and environmental regulation mainly affects government and society. Your relationship with these key stakeholders will ultimately determine the value that you create for your shareholders.

This chapter focuses on the impact of product liability and how you, as a manager, can use the law to seize competitive advantage. In following the Manager's Legal Plan, the chapter will show how product liability concerns can be reframed as opportunities to meet customer needs through new product development.

■ The Impact of Product Liability

Product liability is an especially controversial topic because its impact spreads beyond companies to consumers and society.

Impact of Product Liability on Companies

Product liability as we know it today is the result of changes in the law over the last third of the twentieth century. These changes have left in their wake the bankruptcy of a large number of companies, including industrial giants such as Johns Manville Corporation, A. H. Robins Co., and Dow Corning Corp. The bankrupt Johns Manville Corporation, for example, has settled more than 320,000 asbestos injury claims, has 70,000 pending, and anticipates 500,000 more claims.[1] In 2000 and 2001 alone, eight other companies declared bankruptcy as a result of asbestos claims, including Owens Corning, Babcock and Wilcox, and Armstrong World Industries.

Product liability is front-page news, as companies manufacturing tires, breast implants, tobacco, and a wide variety of other products face lawsuits where claims can exceed a hundred billion dollars. Less well publicized is the impact of product liability on smaller companies that are forced out of business because they cannot compete effectively while paying high product liability insurance premiums. Few people know about Havir Manufacturing, a small punch press manufacturer that was based in St. Paul, Minnesota. Havir was doing fine until, in one year, its product liability insurance premium jumped 1900 percent, which equaled 10 percent of the company's sales. The company could not afford to stay in business. As a result, the company auctioned off its equipment and laid off its workers.[2]

For companies that survive, product liability costs can be oppressive. Acmat Corporation, which was in the asbestos removal business, saw its insurance premium jump in one year from $300,000 for $10 million, while its coverage dropped from $10 million to $6 million. The firm bought the insurance, which it needed to bid on public jobs.[3]

Impact of Product Liability on Consumers

From a consumer perspective, product liability is seen as necessary to force companies to act responsibly in manufacturing and selling products. The consumer perspective is often revealed in the size of jury awards. For instance, Patricia Anderson purchased a used Chevrolet Malibu. While she was driving home from a Christmas Eve church service with her four children, the car was rear-ended by a speeding drunk driver. Anderson escaped serious injury but the four children, sitting in the back seat, were horribly disfigured when the gas tank erupted in flames. Anderson sued General Motors and, in a 1999 trial, the jury held the company liable for $107 million in compensatory damages and another $4.8 billion in punitive damages. A judge later ruled that the punitive damage award was excessive and reduced the amount to "only" $1.09 billion.

The large jury award was based in part on a finding that General Motors wanted to reduce costs by placing the gas tank under the trunk, where it was vulnerable to rupture. An internal GM memorandum concluded that placing the gas tank in a different location would cost $8.59 more per car. In another internal memorandum, a young GM engineer did a "value analysis," which assumed a maximum of five hundred deaths per year in GM cars and a "value" of $200,000 per death. Multiplying five hundred times $200,000 and dividing the result by the number of GM cars on the road (41 million) the engineer came up with a cost per automobile of $2.40, which was less than the $8.59 cost of relocating the fuel tank.[4]

The General Motors case illustrates the controversial nature of product liability. Why should the company have to pay for injuries that were triggered by an accident caused by a speeding drunk driver? Did the memo written by the young engineer actually influence company decisions? Did the placement of the gas tank under the trunk create greater danger than placement in other locations? What is the safety record of the Malibu compared to other cars?

Though these are legitimate questions, it is also important to keep in mind that managers wear two product liability hats. In your role as manager, you are concerned about the impact of product liability on your company. But as a consumer, you want safe products for yourself and your loved ones. The two hats are illustrated by a case in Texas. A forty-two-year-old attorney who specialized in defending companies in product liability cases went hunting with two judges and his sixteen-year-old son. After the hunt, the son entered the car holding a high-powered Remington rifle. One of the judges suggested that he unload the gun. The son released the safety, which was necessary to unload the rifle. The gun fired, wounding the father and leaving him paralyzed from the waist down. The father proceeded to sue Remington, claiming that it should not be necessary to release the safety to unload a rifle. The company settled by paying him $6.8 million.[5]

In another case, an attorney with Venezuela's largest law firm represented Ford Motor Co. and tire maker Bridgestone/

Firestone. His daughter and son-in-law sustained serious injuries and their nanny was killed in an accident allegedly caused by a defective tire on their Ford Explorer. The attorney proceeded to drop the companies as clients and is now leading efforts to sue the companies in the United States.[6]

Impact of Product Liability on Society

Beyond the impact of product liability on individual companies and consumers is the concern that product liability might inhibit innovation and new product development. For example, a Conference Board study concluded, on the basis of responses from CEOs of 264 companies, that 47 percent had discontinued product lines and 39 percent had decided not to introduce new products because of product liability. Over 40 percent of the CEOs indicated that product liability has had a major impact on their ability to compete.[7] An article in the *Economist* refers to product liability as an innovation tax that "dissuades companies from selling their wares in America, prompts them to withdraw safe and effective products, and may even stop research altogether."[8]

■ Apply the Manager's Legal Plan to Product Liability

Product liability is clearly a controversial topic with broad impact. As a manager, you should keep in mind that product liability is not targeted toward your company; the law applies to your competitors as well. The companies that best manage product liability risks will have a better opportunity to reduce costs and position themselves to develop superior products. The four-step Manager's Legal Plan introduced in Chapter One illustrates how you can compete effectively by minimizing product liability risk.

Step One: Understand the Legal Elements of Product Liability

Your CEO has just called you with a message that will change your life for several months or years and perhaps have a permanent impact on your career: "One of our customers has just filed a product liability lawsuit against us." A more chilling version of this message is: "Our customers have filed a product liability class action against the company."

The first step in using the law to seize competitive advantage—and something that you will do instinctively—is to discuss the case with the company's attorney. During this conversation, you will want to proceed directly to the bottom-line questions: What is the customer's version of the story? How much does the customer claim in damages? What are our chances of winning the case? What would it take to settle?

These are all important questions and, in a world where your time is limited, it is tempting to go no further in the conversation with your lawyer. To use the law to seize competitive advantage, however, you must dig deeper. Specifically, you should ask the lawyer to describe the legal basis for the customer's claim. The explanation does not have to be deeply theoretical or technical. Instead, the attorney should be able to describe the law at the level of a judge's instruction to a jury, but in business terms rather than legal terms. Through an understanding of the law, you will have a foundation for proceeding to the next three steps: reacting to the case, developing business strategies and solutions to prevent future legal problems, and reframing the legal problem as a business opportunity for competitive advantage.

The concept of product liability as described in the business media and popular press is too vague and amorphous to be useful in your quest for competitive advantage. As your attorney will explain, "product liability" is an umbrella term that covers three types of defects that can lead to liability: design defects, manufacturing defects, and marketing defects. In many cases a plaintiff will assert all three of these claims, depicted in Figure 2.1, in one case.

Design Defects

Your company is responsible for injuries resulting from defective product design. Your duties in designing a product are governed by reasonableness: Is the design reasonable given your customers' foreseeable uses of the product? Courts recognize that requiring your company to develop a perfectly safe product is often unrealistic. For example, automakers have the ability to design cars that would virtually eliminate personal injuries in automobile accidents. But what would these cars look like? Probably a lot like Sherman tanks. These tank-like cars would be inefficient (with mileage measured in gallons to the mile rather than miles to the gallon), unattractive, prohibitively expensive, and slow. In short, no one would buy them.

As a result, most courts have adopted a balancing test that considers, on one hand, the risks associated with a product and on the other the benefits (or utility) of the product. The test was summarized by the Supreme Court of Georgia in a case involving a nine-year-old child who died after eating rat poison.[9] The poison did not contain a bitter element that would deter consumption by humans or cause them to vomit if the poison were

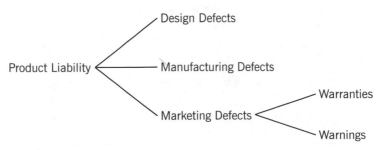

Figure 2.1. Product Liability.

swallowed by mistake. The court first noted that the case involved a design—rather than a manufacturing or marketing—defect. The court then observed that a risk-utility analysis represents the "overwhelming consensus" on the law of defective design: "This risk-utility analysis incorporates the concept of 'reasonableness,' i.e., whether the manufacturer acted reasonably in choosing a particular product design, given the probability and seriousness of the risk posed by the design, the usefulness of the product in that condition, and the burden on the manufacturer to take the necessary steps to eliminate the risk." After reviewing numerous sources, the court developed a list of general factors that are considered in a risk-utility analysis. These factors are presented in question format in Exhibit 2.1. Because these factors were not considered in the original trial (where the parents had prevailed), the Supreme Court of Georgia decided that a new trial was necessary.

Exhibit 2.1. Questions Considered in Risk-Utility Analysis.

1. How useful is the product?
2. Does the design create serious dangers?
3. Is injury likely?
4. Is the danger avoidable?
5. Does the customer have an ability to avoid the danger?
6. What is the state of the art (at time of manufacture)?
7. Can the danger be eliminated without impairing the utility of the product or making it prohibitively expensive?
8. Can the losses sustained by injured customers be spread through higher prices or insurance?
9. Are alternative designs feasible, taking into account cost and adverse effects of the alternative?
10. What are the benefits of the product—for example, appearance, attractiveness, usefulness for multiple purposes, and convenience?

Source: Banks v. *ICI,* Supreme Court of Georgia, 1994.

Manufacturing Defects

Manufacturers, like other defendants, are liable for carelessness (in legal terms, negligence) that results in injury to others. But over the last half of the twentieth century, American courts crafted an additional theory of liability—called strict liability—that makes it much easier for an injured consumer to win a case against a manufacturer. Under this theory, businesses that sell defective products that injure consumers are liable even though they exercise "all possible care" in preparing and selling the product. In other words, the consumer no longer has to prove that the manufacturer was negligent and the manufacturer can no longer successfully defend a lawsuit by asserting that it exercised all care humanly possible in producing the product.

Why would courts turn the business world upside down by fashioning this rule of strict liability? Within the business community there is a feeling that the law is based on the ability of businesses to pay damage awards because they have "deep pockets." Judges and legal scholars, however, claim that the law is designed to shift losses from one person (the injured consumer) to society in general. This loss-shifting occurs when manufacturers raise prices after incurring product liability costs. As one scholar observed: "[Strict liability] is not a 'deep pocket' theory but rather a 'risk-bearing economic' theory. The assumption is that the manufacturer can shift the costs of accidents to purchasers for use by charging higher prices for the costs of products."[10]

The cost-shifting aspect of product liability is illustrated by a case involving a high school student who was paralyzed after his spinal cord was severed while he was playing football. His lawsuit against the helmet manufacturer, Riddell, resulted in a judgment of $5.3 million. Riddell's insurance company proceeded to raise the company's annual product liability insurance premiums from $40,000 to $1.5 million. Riddell responded by raising the price of helmets over the next few years by 33 percent, virtually all of which was attributed to product liability costs.[11]

Football teams faced with higher helmet prices undoubtedly raised the price of tickets and advertising so that ultimately the cost fell on consumers. In other words, the cost of the accident was spread among a large number of consumers rather than falling entirely on the player and his family.

One problem with the theory in the real world of business is that many companies, unable to raise prices enough to reflect product liability costs, are forced out of business. At one time twenty companies manufactured football helmets. Only two remain today.[12]

Another problem with the theory is that a hidden tax is imposed on consumers. According to an article in *Forbes,* this product liability tax "is levied on virtually everything we buy, sell, and use. This tax costs American companies, individuals and local governments at least $80 billion a year, and some estimate as much as $300 billion. It accounts for 30 percent of the price of a stepladder and for over 95 percent of the price of childhood vaccines."[13] Another source estimates that litigation adds 2.5 percent to the cost of a new product.[14] A friend who recently purchased a $75 football helmet for his son in junior high school reported that a sticker on the helmet noted that $25 of the price went toward product liability costs—a 50 percent tax!

Marketing Defects

Two types of marketing defects can lead to product liability. As depicted in Figure 2.2, liability can result either from express or implied warranties that you provide to your customers or from your failure to warn customers of hidden dangers associated with the product.

Warranties. Your warranty liability is based on statements— called *express warranties*—that you make to consumers. When you state a fact, make a promise, or describe your product, you

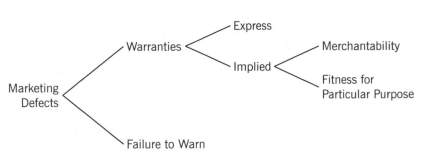

Figure 2.2. **Marketing Defects.**

are giving express warranties. The information that you provide does not have to be distributed with the product and does not have to use the word *warranty* to create liability.

For example, an advertisement can create an express warranty. At one time cigarette companies emphasized the safety of smoking with ads like those in Exhibit 2.2. The U.S. Supreme Court has ruled that a smoker could sue tobacco companies because, through these ads, cigarette companies gave express warranties that cigarettes are safe.[15]

Even when your company does not give express warranties, the law automatically gives purchasers two warranties, called *implied warranties.* One of these implied warranties is the warranty of merchantability. With this warranty, your company promises to the purchaser that your products are of average quality and fit for ordinary purposes. For example, a customer sued Goodyear Tire & Rubber, claiming that the company sold faulty rubber hosing that was used to build heating systems in the floors of houses. According to an article in the *Wall Street Journal,* a jury decided that "Goodyear didn't breach its 'implied warranty of merchantability.'" In other words, the hosing was of average quality and fit for ordinary purposes (in this case, fit for use in heating systems).[16]

The second implied warranty is the warranty of fitness for a particular purpose. Your company gives this warranty in situations

Exhibit 2.2. Tobacco Advertisements.

"PLAY SAFE Smoke Chesterfield"

"NOSE, THROAT, and Accessory Organs Not Adversely Affected by Smoking Chesterfields"

"[Chesterfields are] *entirely safe for the mouth*"

"CHESTERFIELD FIRST TO GIVE YOU SCIENTIFIC FACTS IN SUPPORT OF SMOKING"

"[L & M filters are] just what the doctor ordered"

Source: Cippolone v. Liggett Group, Inc., U.S. Court of Appeals (3rd Circuit), 1990.

where you know that the buyer needs your product for a particular purpose and that the buyer is relying on your skill and judgment in providing a product that will meet the buyer's needs.

Warnings and Failure to Warn. Your company has a legal duty to warn customers about dangers associated with foreseeable uses of your product and to provide instructions that explain how to use the product safely. The list of dangers includes product features that could lead to physical harm. In one case, a doctor replaced the heart valve of a patient named Bravman with a mechanical valve. The mechanical valve made a loud noise that, in some patients, could be heard in a quiet room from as far away as twenty feet away. When Bravman sued the manufacturer, the court decided that there was no design defect (because the usefulness of the product outweighed the noise problems) or manufacturing defect.

However, the court determined that the manufacturer could be held liable for failing to warn the patient of the noise problem. There was evidence that the manufacturer knew that its mechanical valves were noisy. Other patients had complained and one had attempted suicide because of the noise. In this case, the patient alleged that he had lost sleep, become despondent, and been forced to take early retirement because of the noise.

The court concluded that: "Unlike the purely psychological terror suffered by the protagonist in Edgar Allan Poe's 'The Tell-Tale Heart,' Bravman's complaint, that his artificial heart valve creates excessive noise that prevents him from sleeping, among other things, is objectively verifiable."[17]

Your Personal Liability

Your company will be liable if the plaintiff can prove any one of the three types of defects: design, manufacturing, or marketing. But does company liability also result in personal liability for your role in manufacturing or distributing a product?

The answer contains good news and bad news. The good news is that plaintiffs typically sue only the company because the company is considered the seller of the product under manufacturing defect and warranty theories.

The bad news is that managers face potential criminal liability under a fairly new law adopted in California. The California Corporate Criminal Liability Act is better known by its informal name, the "Be a Manager and Go to Jail" law. Under this law, a manager who works for a company that does business in California must report serious product defects to a state agency within a limited period of time or face a prison term of up to three years.

Armed with an understanding of the three types of product defects that are collectively known as product liability, you are now ready to move to the next step: flight or fight.

Step Two: React to the Product Liability Problem Through Flight or Fight

As discussed in Chapter One, the traditional reaction to legal problems like product liability lawsuits has been either flight or fight. For reasons discussed below, the flight option is no longer realistic in a global economy. The fight option includes two possibilities, fighting for product liability law reform and fighting a specific lawsuit, both of which will be explored later in the chapter.

Flight

Until the mid-1980s, when other countries began to adopt U.S.-style strict liability, it was felt that companies could escape the impact of product liability law by moving operations and sales to other countries. But this option was not feasible for companies that intended to market their products in the rich consumer market of the United States, as they could not escape liability by arguing that their products were made in another country.

Increasingly, the option of moving operations is not feasible even for companies that intend to manufacture and market their product solely outside the United States. As noted in Chapter One, the law—like the economy—has become globalized and product liability has spread to Europe and Asia. Countries in the European Union were the first to adopt U.S.-style strict liability, and they were soon followed by countries in the Pacific Rim region, including Australia, China, the Philippines, and Japan.

In some cases, product liability law in other countries is harsher on companies and managers than the American version. In Vietnam, the product liability law provides that a manager who fails to meet quality standards "should be punished by up to one year of re-education."[18] In China, consumers filed more than five hundred thousand lawsuits annually during the three years following adoption of a new product law. According to a 1997 *Wall Street Journal* article: "Product liability, a concept practically unheard of here 20 years ago, has caught the attention of China's consumers—and they're applying it with a vengeance. For decades, the Chinese had little recourse when they were shocked, burned or dismembered by shoddy state-produced goods. Now they can sue."[19] The same article notes a unique feature of Chinese law: newspaper articles can be introduced as evidence. Media campaigns result in headlines such as: "Is a

Chinese Life Worth Less Than a Foreign Life?" and "A Needle in My Father's Heart."

Fight
Your product liability battles will take two forms. First, you can fight for reform of product liability law. Second, you can fight individual lawsuits filed against your company.

Fight for Law Reform. Companies upset over the impact of product liability have pushed for reform of product liability law at the state and federal level. This fight has been successful to some extent at the state level, where laws have been enacted that place caps on certain types of damages, such as damages for pain and suffering and punitive damages. Other laws provide that if a product does not cause injury within a set time period, the manufacturer is not liable. However, supporters of law reform have been unsuccessful in achieving a return from strict liability to a fault-based system of liability.

Although attempts to reform product liability law may be laudable, reform efforts should not overshadow strategies to achieve competitive advantage within the legal system currently in place. After all, legal systems do not target your company; your competitors must play by the same rules. Law reform will simply move you and your competitors to a different field without creating a competitive advantage for your company.

Fight Individual Product Liability Lawsuits. As discussed earlier in the chapter, it is likely that your customers will claim any or all of the three types of defects in their lawsuits against your company: design defects, manufacturing defects, and marketing defects. The strategy that you and your attorney will develop to defend a lawsuit will focus on these claims. Specifically, you will attempt to prove that there were no defects in your design, manufacture, and marketing of the product. For example, you might argue that the product was properly designed under the risk-utility analysis, the product was not defective when it left the manufacturing plant (a common argument in cases where customers alter products), and there were no marketing defects because the product did not violate the "merchantability" warranty (that is, it was of average quality).

A key issue at the heart of most product liability cases is whether the product was defective. For instance, in one case a company delivered a stack of produce to a grocery store. After a produce manager removed a box of bananas from the top of the stack, a six-inch banana spider leaped from the stack onto the manager's hand and bit him. He later died of heart failure. His widow sued the company that sold the produce claiming that the bananas were defective. The court decided in favor of the company on the grounds that the product was not defective. The bananas "were edible and saleable. In these circumstances, neither the doctrine of strict liability nor breach of implied warranty of fitness applies."[20]

After winning a case like this, there is a tendency to breathe a sigh of relief and return to normal business activities. In a business world operating at Internet speed, there is little time to savor victory or reflect on its causes. But is this case really a victory for the company when all costs are considered? Beyond costs directly associated with the litigation, such as lawyers' and expert witness fees, there is the cost of management time spent on gathering documents, meetings with lawyers, and giving depositions. There are also opportunity costs associated with losing time that could be spent on business development. An even greater cost can be the loss in market share resulting from negative publicity that surrounds lawsuits. As a result it is important to exercise discipline after a victory (or loss) in court by moving to Step Three, the proactive search for business strategies and solutions that will reduce or prevent recurring product liability costs.

Step Three: Develop Business Strategies and Solutions That Minimize Product Liability

The search for business strategies and solutions requires a long-term perspective on product liability and its impact on your company. The results of this search may vary by company or industry, but there are three fundamental business approaches to minimizing the consequences of product liability in a manner that will allow you to seize competitive advantage: a strategic approach, an organizational approach, and an operations approach. These approaches are depicted in Figure 2.3.

Strategic Approach

The strategic approach focuses on this fundamental business question: Should you continue to make products that subject the company to potential liability? In answering this question, you may decide to drop products on the basis of your litigation experience and the size of damage awards. But through this knee-jerk analysis, you may lose significant business opportunities.

Figure 2.3. Business Solutions for Product Liability.

For a deeper strategic analysis, you should return to the legal elements of product liability discussed earlier. One of the key elements is strict liability, which replaced traditional fault-based liability. Under strict liability, the company is liable when it sells a defective product, whether or not the company was negligent. This rule is based on the theory that the company is simply an intermediary that adjusts prices and passes on the product liability costs to consumers. With this theory in mind, your strategic analysis should focus on whether your company can indeed pass on its product liability costs to consumers (as the theory predicts) or whether it must bear the costs because of an inability to raise prices. In other words, the analysis should focus on who ultimately pays, rather than on whether there is liability.

To illustrate this analysis, let's assume that you work for a company in the industry that has incurred the highest product liability costs—tobacco. Settlements and jury verdicts have pushed the product liability of the industry to hundreds of billions of dollars. Faced with a portion of this liability, your company might easily be tempted to drop cigarettes as a product.

But a deeper analysis would focus on whether this liability can be passed on to customers. For example, after tobacco companies agreed to a $206 billion settlement with forty-six states in 1998, the companies raised their prices by 76 cents a pack, which allowed them to fund the settlement despite a 7 percent drop in cigarette consumption. And it is estimated that companies can fund the $144.9 billion awarded by a jury in a 2000 case by increasing prices by another 35 cents. As noted in a *Wall Street Journal* article: "Where does the [state settlement] money come from? Generally speaking, not the bottom line. . . . Viewed from the consumer perspective, the settlements effectively transfer vast wealth from smokers to states and lawyers on both sides."[21] This analysis, by the way, is not to suggest that companies should manufacture and sell cigarettes, as there are other factors besides an economic analysis that should affect the decision.

Organizational Approach

Once you make the strategic decision to continue a product line, you should review your organizational structure. This review brings into play one of the foundations of capitalism—the concept of limited liability. Under this concept, when you buy stock in a corporation, the most you can lose is your investment. If the company fails and declares bankruptcy, the creditors cannot seize your personal assets. In other words, the company represents a "corporate veil" that protects you from liability.

This concept also applies when one company (call it "Parent") buys shares in another company ("Subsidiary"). If Subsidiary fails, Parent is not liable for its debts. This creates an opportunity to isolate your product liability risks in a subsidiary. Your lawyers will create the subsidiary as an independent corporation. Your company, the parent corporation, will typically own 100 percent of the subsidiary's stock. If, in the worst-case scenario, there are major product liability damage awards against the subsidiary, the parent company will lose its investment in the subsidiary but will not be liable beyond this investment.

There are exceptions to the principle of limited liability that are especially important to managers. A parent corporation that is directly involved with its subsidiary's product development risks direct liability. For example, Dow Corning is an independent corporation owned by two shareholders, Dow Chemical Co. (50 percent) and Corning Inc. (50 percent). Dow Corning filed for bankruptcy after plaintiffs filed thousands of product liability lawsuits in which they claimed injuries resulting from silicone breast implants. Normally, the maximum amount that Dow and Corning would have at risk would be their investment in Dow Corning. But, in over fourteen thousand lawsuits filed against Dow, plaintiffs claimed that the parent should be held liable because years ago it participated in Dow Corning business.[22] Corning, which did not participate in testing silicone, has not faced similar claims.

Another exception to the limited liability principle is especially common. If the parent corporation does not treat the subsidiary as an independent corporation, courts will "pierce the corporate veil" and hold the parent liable to the subsidiary's creditors. For example, several years ago world-class driver Mark Donohue was killed when a tire manufactured by Goodyear blew out during a race. When his estate sued Goodyear in the United States, the company argued that, because the tire was manufactured by its British subsidiary, the lawsuit should be filed in England. But the trial judge allowed the case to proceed against the parent company on the grounds that Goodyear dominated the subsidiary rather than treating it as an independent corporation. A comment on the case in *Forbes* observed, "One of the reasons companies set up subsidiaries, in fact, is to use the corporate form to limit legal liability. For the same reason that you can't sue GM shareholders if a Chevrolet's brakes fail, you can't sue Goodyear if a tire made by its subsidiary has a blowout. . . . [But] companies get into trouble over the question of whether they have dominated subsidiaries to the extent that they are indistinguishable from the parent."[23]

Courts are also inclined to pierce the corporate veil when the subsidiary is inadequately capitalized, when the parent describes the subsidiary as a department or division (rather than as a corporation), when the subsidiary does not follow normal legal requirements such as holding regular board meetings, and when the parent uses the subsidiary's property as its own.

The message for managers is clear. Your attorneys will be able to incorporate a subsidiary that can be used to manufacture products that carry significant product liability risks. But to be protected by the corporate veil that the attorneys have created, you must allow the subsidiary to operate as an independent entity.

Operations Approach
In addition to considering organizational structure, your decision to continue a product line should include a review of operations.

Your operations approach to minimizing product liability costs should relate to the three types of defects: design, manufacturing, and marketing. The importance of eliminating manufacturing defects is obvious and has already received considerable attention as a result of quality programs adopted by companies around the world. This chapter will focus instead on a process for eliminating design and marketing defects, which are especially common forms of product liability. The design and marketing process has six key steps.

1. *Form a product review team.* In assembling product review teams, you may be inclined to invite participants with engineering backgrounds who understand product design. The risk is that engineers, while bright and logical, may be too focused on the product's intended purpose and may be uncomfortable thinking outside the box about how "real people" (that is, non-engineers) actually use products. For reasons discussed in the next section, your product review team should include representatives from functions throughout the company. You should also include potential customers on the team and invite them to describe how they might use your product.

2. *Identify foreseeable uses.* You may recall from the earlier discussion of design and marketing defects that you must design the product and develop warnings based on the foreseeable ways in which customers use your product, rather than just on the ways that you intend that they use the product. Thus the team should consider all possible ways that customers might use your product. For example, I have led simulations in which product review teams composed of experienced managers create a list of possible uses of a hairdryer. Within a matter of seconds, team members are able to think of uses similar to the list in Exhibit 2.3. Informal brainstorming should, of course, be supplemented with a review and analysis of claims relating to similar products.

3. *Identify risks.* The team should identify risks associated with foreseeable uses. For instance, in reviewing the list

Exhibit 2.3. **Foreseeable Uses of a Hairdryer.**

People use hairdryers to:

Dry hair
Dry clothes
Start barbecues
Shrink plastic
Dry glue and paint
Defrost refrigerators
Thaw frozen pipes
Dry pets
Remove stickers
Dry fingernail polish
Dust
Defrost locks

in Exhibit 2.3, you might decide that there are risks associated with using the hairdryer to dry glue and paint but that using the hairdryer to defrost locks creates no danger.

4. *Redesign the product.* The team should determine whether the product can be redesigned to eliminate the risk. In considering design issues, the team should conduct a risk-utility analysis that focuses on the questions summarized in Exhibit 2.1.

5. *Develop warnings.* The team should develop warnings (and safety instructions) for the risks that cannot be eliminated through redesign. In my experience with product review teams in simulations involving senior managers, I have observed that team members tend to skip discussion of redesign and move directly to the development of warnings once risks have been identified. This is a mistake—a court may not allow warnings as a defense if a safer design is available. For example, an individual suffered brain injury when a 16-inch Goodrich tire exploded as he attempted to mount it on a 16.5-inch rim. A prominent warning label attached to the tire contained warnings (see Exhibit 2.4) in red and yellow highlights and also a drawing that

Exhibit 2.4. Warning Label Attached to Tire.

DANGER

NEVER MOUNT A 16" SIZE DIAMETER TIRE ON A 16.5" RIM. Mounting a
16" tire on a 16.5" rim can cause severe injury or death. While it is possible
to pass a 16" diameter tire over the lip or flange of a 16.5" size diameter rim,
it cannot position itself against the rim flange. If an attempt is made to seat the
bead by inflating the tire, the tire bead will break with explosive force.

NEVER inflate a tire which is lying on the floor or other flat surface. Always
use a tire mounting machine with a hold-down device or safety cage or bolt to
vehicle axle.

NEVER inflate to seat beads without using an extension hose with gauge and
clip-on chuck.

NEVER stand, lean or reach over the assembly during inflation.
Failure to comply with these safety precautions can cause the bead to break
and the assembly to burst with sufficient force to cause serious injury or death.

Source: Uniroyal Goodrich Tire Co. v. Martinez, Supreme Court of Texas, 1998.

depicted an exploding tire throwing a worker into the air. The
worker had ignored all of the warnings. In a lawsuit against
Goodyear, the Supreme Court of Texas affirmed a jury award of
$5.5 million in damages. The court noted that "a product may
be unreasonably dangerous because of a defect in manufacturing, design, or marketing." In this case, because there was evidence that the tire was defectively designed, the warning label
did not excuse the design defect. As the court noted (quoting a
legal authority): *"Warnings are not, however, a substitute for the pro-
vision of a reasonably safe design."* (The italics were added by the
court for emphasis.)[24]

6. *Review warranties.* Finally, the team should determine
what, if any, warranties should accompany the product. Your
company can avoid liability for express warranties simply by
not giving them. In marketing your products you can also disclaim express warranties, although the disclaimer will not work
if it conflicts with an express warranty. For example, a warranty

from a clothing manufacturer stated that the company would replace a product if it did not provide "one year of normal wear." Below this statement, in small type, was a disclaimer that the warranty would not apply if the garment were "worn out." If tested in court, the one-year warranty should prevail over the disclaimer.

You can also disclaim the warranties that are automatically provided by law—the implied warranties discussed earlier in this chapter. For example, to disclaim the implied warranty of merchantability, the disclaimer must mention the word *merchantability* and, if in writing, must be conspicuous. The implied warranty of fitness for a particular purpose can be disclaimed through a conspicuous disclaimer that is in writing. For examples of disclaimers, simply visit your favorite Web site. Chances are that you will find disclaimers similar to those found on the Amazon.com Web site (in print twice as large as other print on the Web site):

AMAZON.COM DISCLAIMS ALL WARRANTIES,
EXPRESS OR IMPLIED, INCLUDING, BUT NOT LIMITED
TO, IMPLIED WARRANTIES OF MERCHANTABILITY
AND FITNESS FOR A PARTICULAR PURPOSE.

This section has examined three business approaches—strategic, organizational, and operational—that you can use to seize competitive advantage by reducing or eliminating product liability risks. You are now ready to climb to the balcony in an attempt to reframe product liability as a business opportunity rather than solely a legal issue. This attempt may enable you to use the law to achieve growth through new product development.

Step Four: Climb to the Balcony— Reframe Product Liability as a Business Opportunity

When you climb to the balcony to view product liability in perspective, the results may vary depending on your product line. But there is at least one perspective that should prove useful across product lines. This perspective relates to the six-step new product process that is used to reduce liability for defective design and to develop warnings for those design defects that cannot be eliminated.

When running simulations of this process with senior managers, I have encountered considerable hostility toward a feature of the law that allows customers to recover for injuries that result when they use products for purposes other than those intended by the manufacturer. Often the process brings to mind stories managers have heard or experiences they have had with their own customers' misuse of products. Some of these stories are urban myths (or at least I cannot locate them in published case reports). These include stories of the cat that exploded when its owner attempted to dry it in a microwave and the woman who used contraceptive jelly on her toast every morning and still became pregnant.[25]

But other stories—often drawn from the executives' own experience—are true. For example, a person driving a Ford Pinto struck a horse. The horse flipped onto the roof above the windshield. The impact caused the roof to collapse, instantly killing the driver's wife. Ford Motor Company was held liable for a design defect because, among other reasons, "the accident and the manner of injury were not unforeseeable."[26]

When considering a case like this, there is a tendency to criticize judges who push the boundaries of foreseeability or customers who misuse products. While criticism may be justified in certain cases, by focusing on the legal aspects of product liability, you may overlook significant business opportunities. For example, let's return to the hairdryer example. You might consider most of the uses in Exhibit 2.3 to be examples of customer stupidity, as customers should not use hairdryers for purposes other than drying hair.

But is this the attitude of a manager in a customer-focused, market-driven company? What are your customers trying to tell you when they use hairdryers for a wide variety of purposes?

The common theme in the list is that customers need warm air. They do not have access to products on the market that provide warm air and consequently must use hairdryers for this purpose. Companies that move beyond a purely legal focus in their design review (that is, beyond a focus on developing designs that minimize liability) and use information from the process to develop new products will achieve competitive advantage. As legendary General Motors president Alfred Sloan once stated in a letter to shareholders: "To discuss Consumer Research as a functional activity would give an erroneous impression. In its broad implications it is more in the nature of an OPERATING PHILOSOPHY, which to be fully effective, must extend through all phases of the business . . . [and] serve the customer in ways in which the customer wants to be served."[27]

"All phases of the business" includes the "law phase" of the business. In other words, law should be used not only to control costs but also to generate new product ideas. As a leading management consultant—a person who founded one of the top international consulting firms and has played key roles in the development of two others—once told me, the key to strategy is listening to customers.

Listening to your customers through the legal information they provide extends beyond new product development. Once your product is on the market, it becomes important to listen to your customers through their complaints about your product, their warranty claims, and their lawsuits against your company. This form of data mining is especially useful in the continuing redesign of your products in order to maintain competitive advantage.

The listening process also extends to liability related to services that you provide with your products. For instance, at one time Domino's Pizza guaranteed pizza delivery within thirty minutes or customers would receive a discount. After several traffic accidents involving Domino's drivers the company faced public criticism and lawsuits.

If you were a Domino's executive, how would you respond to this problem? One response might be to require continuous training of your drivers. But it is likely that training would be costly and might not significantly reduce the number of accidents. Better screening of potential drivers would probably lead to the same result. Another approach would be to drop your thirty-minute guarantee. But you might lose a significant marketing advantage, as well as the opportunity to provide the best service to your customers.

Domino's opted for the last approach, dropping the thirty-minute guarantee. But in doing so, rather than complaining about the negative impact of the law on customer service, the company asked the question suggested by Alfred Sloan: What do our customers really want? The company discovered that, while customers want their pizza delivered as soon as possible, an important reason behind this desire for speedy delivery is that they want their pizza to be served hot. The solution? A new service-enhancing product—a bag that contains heating coils that keeps the pizza hot until delivery.

CHAPTER SUMMARY

This chapter has applied the four-step Manager's Legal Plan for achieving competitive advantage to one of the most controversial and complex issues affecting you and your customers: product liability. It first examined the impact of product liability on your company, on consumers, and on society. The chapter then proceeded through the four steps of the Manager's Legal Plan:

Step One. Understand the legal elements of product liability. Product liability is a combination of claims. A typical case includes claims of design defect, which involves an analysis of your product's risk and utility; manufacturing defect, which today is based on the theory of strict liability and on the assumption that liability can be passed on to the consumer through higher prices; and marketing defect, which might arise from breach of warranty or failure to warn.

Step Two. React to product liability through flight or fight. Of the two traditional response mechanisms that are embedded in our genetic code, flight is rarely possible because the theory of strict liability has spread beyond U.S. borders to Europe and Asia. The product liability fight takes two forms. First, there is the fight for law reform, which has achieved modest success but does not provide competitive advantage to any one company. Second, the fight in individual cases will focus on defending against the three claims summarized in Step One. At the most fundamental level, you must fight to prove that your product was not defective.

Step Three. Develop business strategies and solutions that minimize product liability. There is a tendency for managers to move on to other concerns when the product liability fight is over. But the key to using the law for competitive advantage is to move instead to this third step, which might minimize future claims by transforming the way you do business. This involves three approaches. First, the strategic approach uses the theory of strict liability to decide whether to add or drop product lines. Second, the organizational approach focuses on the use of subsidiaries to isolate serious product liability risks. Third, the operational approach uses a design and marketing process to identify foreseeable uses of your product, redesign the product, and develop appropriate warnings.

Step Four. Go to the balcony to reframe product liability as a business opportunity. This last step covers ways to use the design review process not only to minimize liability but also to generate growth through new product development. The process represents an important form of consumer research in any company that aspires to be market driven and focused on customer needs.

Questions to Consider

1. Have you isolated major product liability risks in a subsidiary?
2. Do you use the six-step design and marketing process to develop appropriate designs and warnings?
3. Do you use information about customers' foreseeable uses of your product to identify customer needs?
4. Do you use data gathered from customer complaints, warranty claims, and lawsuits to develop new products?

Create Competitive Advantage Through Your Employees

Workers' Compensation, Wrongful Discharge, and Sexual Harassment

The focus of Chapter Two is on the most controversial and expensive legal issue affecting your customers—product liability. The chapter uses the four-step Manager's Legal Plan to illustrate how product liability costs can be controlled and how a design and marketing process can be used as a source of consumer research and product innovation.

Your employees are just as important as your customers to your goal of achieving competitive advantage. In the past, an organization's assets were measured in terms of land, buildings, and equipment. In today's information-based economy, the intellectual capital created by your employees is your key asset.

Your ability to find and retain the best employees through attractive compensation and work-life balance programs while at the same time controlling employment costs is a critical element in achieving competitive advantage.

The legal relationship between employer and employee has changed dramatically in recent years. At one time, when unions played a greater role in the workplace, the employment relationship was dominated by collective bargaining agreements. Although these agreements often struck employers as unreasonable and costly, they had the benefit of providing stability. If there was an employment dispute, you went to the contract to determine your rights.

In recent years, a decline in the number of workers covered by collective bargaining agreements has coincided with increased court involvement in determining employee rights. For example, a study of cases filed in federal district court from 1971 to 1991 indicated that employment litigation increased a whopping 430 percent while business litigation (cases filed by Fortune 1000 firms) increased by only 121 percent and personal injury litigation increased by only 17 percent.[1] The increasing intervention by courts in employer-employee matters has created greater uncertainty but also greater opportunity for competitive advantage.

The three legal areas that dominate the employment relationship are captured in the chapter title—workers' compensation, wrongful discharge, and sexual harassment. This chapter will apply the four-step Manager's Legal Plan to these three areas of the law. The discussion will focus especially on workers' compensation, which has the greatest and most pervasive impact on business. But the Manager's Legal Plan will also be used to explore business strategies relating to wrongful discharge and sexual harassment.

■ The Impact of Workers' Compensation on Your Business

Workers' compensation costs increased dramatically toward the end of the twentieth century. In the United States, for example, workers' compensation insurance costs jumped from $5 billion in the mid-1970s to $21 billion in the mid-1980s to $70 billion in the early 1990s.[2] Although many companies gained greater control of these costs in the late 1990s, the National Safety Council estimates that in 1998 the cost of work injuries in the United States exceeded $125 billion—almost triple the combined profits of the top five *Fortune* 500 firms for the same year. According to the NSC, "At work there is a fatal injury every 103 minutes and a disabling injury every 8 seconds."[3] Overall, according to Bureau of Labor Statistics estimates, in 1998 there were 5.9 million workplace injuries and illnesses reported in private industries alone, or 6.7 cases per 100 workers.[4]

Although recent years have seen a drop in workers' compensation costs as a percentage of payroll, costs vary dramatically among companies. For example, a study of Michigan companies concluded that workers' compensation costs at some companies were ten times those of their competitors.[5] A national study of *Fortune* 500 companies determined that from 1988 to 1992, some companies' workers' compensation costs increased as much as 152 percent while in comparable companies costs decreased by up to 26 percent.[6]

The impact on competitive advantage is obvious, because workers' compensation costs have a significant impact on a company's bottom line. As the annual report for the U.S. Postal Service notes, "our bottom line is affected every time an employee is injured and unable to return to work."[7] For example, looking at insurance costs alone, if your company has a poor workers' compensation record you might pay twice the average premium, while your competitor with a good record might pay only 60 percent of the average.[8] If the average premium is $10 million, you would pay a premium of $20 million and your competitor's payments would total only $6 million—a difference of $14 million.

■ Apply the Manager's Legal Plan to Workers' Compensation

The Manager's Legal Plan provides a handy way to examine how workers' compensation costs can be reduced and to explore whether, by climbing the balcony, the legal problem of workers' compensation can be viewed as a business issue that will produce new opportunities for competitive advantage.

Step One: Understand Workers' Compensation Law

To seize competitive advantage you first must understand the fundamentals of the workers' compensation system. The concept of workers' compensation is attributed to German Chancellor Otto von Bismarck. Concerned about the increasing number of accidents resulting from the Industrial Revolution, he created the first workers' compensation system in 1884.[9] The German system was imported by the United States in the early 1900s and is now a standard feature in the law of most states.

Workers' compensation involves a trade-off between employee and employer. Employees receive compensation for injuries at work, including the cost of hospitalization and medical care, lost wages, and death benefits. In return, employees give up the right to sue the company for damages in a traditional personal injury lawsuit. The net result is that the company pays a specified amount for on-the-job injuries, even when it is not at fault, and is protected from lawsuits that might result in large damage awards, even when the company is at fault. Workers' compensation, in other words, is the "exclusive remedy" available to employees injured at work.

Workers' compensation is based on the theory that the financial burdens of injured workers can be shifted to society at large through price increases that reflect employers' costs. According to a campaign slogan, "the cost of the product should bear the blood of the workman."[10]

Not all work-related injuries are compensated under the system. For example, depending on state law, workers may be unable to recover for injuries resulting from a personal fight, horseplay, an intentional self-injury, or intoxication.[11] And employees who are injured as a result of the employer's intentional acts can bypass the system and sue an employer for personal injury damages.

However, these exceptions are often difficult to apply. For instance, Stroh Brewery fired a worker for intoxication on the job. The worker filed a workers' compensation claim against the brewery. He claimed that, although he was predisposed to alcoholism, he only drank three or four bottles of beer on weekends before working for the company. Stroh provided free beer to all employees at a "designated relief area" and the worker's consumption grew to nine to twelve bottles a day. The court eventually decided that he was entitled to compensation. Aggravation of a preexisting disease (here alcoholism) through employment, the court noted, falls within workers' compensation coverage.[12]

In another case, a worker inserted two coins in a coffee machine. When one of the coins became wedged in the machine, the employee gave the machine what the court called a "whack" and in so doing injured his arm. According to an orthopedic surgeon he suffered a 10 percent loss of use of the upper right arm. The Supreme Court of Rhode Island decided that the injury was covered by workers' compensation. The injury occurred at work;

the employee was performing a permitted act (buying coffee); and the fact that he obtained the coffee in an improper manner (by whacking the machine) would not prevent recovery. One judge, however, did observe that the worker's "confrontation with the balky coffee machine qualifies him to join . . . what might be described as the Rhode Island Workers' Compensation Hall of Fame."[13]

While the workers' compensation concept is fairly straightforward, new forms of workplace injuries have placed strains on the system. In the early years of the twentieth century, most claims were based on physical injuries such as amputations and fractures. After World War II, soft tissue injuries—for example, back injury—became more common. More recently, as work has become more mental than physical, claims relating to mental injury have increased.[14]

The evolution of injury claims has resulted in an evolution of workers' compensation law. For example, most states allow compensation when mental stress on the job results in physical injury, such as ulcers. And most states also provide compensation for mental disability that results from physical injury, such as depression following the loss of a hand. But what if the mental claim is not connected with physical injury?

This is the issue faced by a New York court in a case involving a secretary who worked for several years for the head of security of a department store. One morning she found him lying in a pool of blood, where he had fallen after shooting himself in the head. This event triggered what a psychiatrist called an acute depressive reaction. The secretary eventually recovered after hospitalization, psychotherapy, medication, and electroshock treatment. The court allowed workers' compensation, emphasizing that the system "is designed to shift the risk of loss of earning capacity caused by industrial accidents from the worker to industry and ultimately to the consumer."[15]

What if the cause of mental problems is not direct and immediate, as in the secretary's case, but results from general stress on the job? A New York court considered this issue after an NBC employee committed suicide. The court (in following the lead of several other states) decided that the suicide was related to stress on the job.[16] Following top-level management changes, the decedent had to carry a beeper, received many calls at home from the president of NBC, and worked many weekends. He was also given responsibility for an area of the company that had not functioned well for years. In suicide notes to his supervisor and to his wife, he stated that he could no longer face what he perceived as failure. This case, like the others involving the intoxicated worker, the machine whacker, and the depressed secretary, illustrate that the workers' compensation concept is often difficult to apply and is evolving to reflect changes in the nature of work.

Step Two: React to the Workers' Compensation Legal Problem Through Flight or Fight

Once you understand the workers' compensation system, you can react to the legal problems it causes by attempting to flee them. You can also fight—for law reform and through your handling of individual cases.

Flight

Flight to another state is a realistic option when you are faced with workers' compensation problems. Variation in state laws can result in dramatic cost savings. The chairman of Chesebrough-Pond once reported that, over a five-year period, employment at the company's Bass Shoe division in Maine had increased by 40 percent while workers' compensation payments had increased 2,300 percent. He compared operations at the company's Health-tex plants in Maine with plants in Alabama by noting that the company had twice the number of workers in Alabama, but "less than half the workers' compensation costs."[17]

Fight for Law Reform

The threat of losing business has prompted most states to reform workers' compensation law. California reformed its law after a study revealed that the state had lost over 650 manufacturing plants because of the business climate. Intel, for example, decided to build a new plant in New Mexico because a plant in California would cost $80 million more in workers' compensation.[18]

Among the most popular reforms adopted by the states are managed care arrangements to control medical costs; laws and regulations designed to encourage workplace safety, such as increased government inspections; financial incentives that encourage employees to return to work; and restructuring of insurance mechanisms.[19]

While these reforms have improved the workers' compensation system, at least from the employers' perspective, they are not a source of competitive advantage for your firm. You and your competitors play on a level field; law reform has simply improved playing conditions for everyone. There will still be winners and losers on this new field.

Fight Specific Workers' Compensation Cases

You will engage in a standard ritual in fighting specific workers' compensation claims. To experience the ritual from the employer's perspective, put yourself in the shoes of the president of a small manufacturer. To promote good will, your company sponsors a Christmas party that begins in the company offices one afternoon during normal working hours. At the party you distribute paychecks and bonuses. The company provides pizza for the party, along with soda, beer, and whiskey. An employee who "partook of the proverbial Christmas cheer" becomes intoxicated and falls from a third floor window. He fractures his skull and spine and severely damages his left leg, which must be amputated above the knee.

What is your strategy when the employee sues your company or makes a workers' compensation claim? The answer depends on whether your company could be held liable if the employee sued it in a traditional personal injury case. If so, you will want to argue that the case is covered by workers' compensation. Why? Because workers' compensation is the exclusive remedy for injuries at work, which means that the employee cannot recover a huge damage award.

If you are confident that your company is not at fault and would not be held liable in a personal injury case, you will want to argue that the case is not a work-related injury and that you owe nothing to the employee. This was the situation in the Christmas party case. The company argued that the employee was not covered by workers' compensation because work had ended when the accident occurred. The court, however, held that the worker was entitled to workers' compensation benefits. In analyzing the case, the court focused on these questions:

- Was the party held during normal working hours? (Yes.)
- Was attendance expected? (Yes—you would expect employees to attend to pick up their paychecks and bonuses.)
- Did the company expect to benefit from the party? (Yes, the purpose was to promote good will.)
- Did the company pay for the party? (Yes.)[20]

Although the case was decided in Rhode Island, the court did not mention whether the employee qualified for the imaginary Rhode Island Workers' Compensation Hall of Fame, as was the worker who whacked the coffee machine in the case described earlier in this chapter.

In planning your legal strategy, you should also understand workers' compensation strategy from the perspective of employees. To illustrate an employee's strategy, consider the case of a Montana employee who operated a drill press for around fifteen years. Intrigued by a hole in the machine, he finally placed his right forefinger in the hole. The finger was amputated. After his recovery, an inspector asked him what happened. The worker turned on the machine and demonstrated what happened by placing his left forefinger into the hole. The finger was amputated.[21]

While the case report does not indicate what happened in court, it is likely that the employee used a well-defined strategy. First, for the right forefinger, he would claim the automatic payments that are due from the employer under workers' compensation. He would also sue the manufacturer of the drill press, claiming product liability. (Only employers are protected by the exclusive remedy feature of workers' compensation.) As a workers' compensation attorney once noted, "the first thing that [an employee's attorney looks] at when an injured worker comes in for help is 'Can we get out of the workers' comp system . . . ?'" He explained that damages for a worker who loses an eye would probably be ten times greater outside the system.[22]

For the second finger, there would also be a product liability claim against the manufacturer, and it is likely that the worker would also sue the employer for intentional injury. As noted earlier, intentional injuries are exceptions to the workers' compensation system. The worker would attempt to prove that the employer's failure to cover the hole was so serious that it was equivalent to an intentional act. A claim that injuries were caused intentionally can be especially devastating because they might not be covered by your insurance and might result in punitive damages.

Typical employer and employee strategies are summarized in Exhibit 3.1. As this exhibit notes, when your company is at fault, you will argue that the case falls within the workers' compensation system, in which case the employee will be unable to

Exhibit 3.1. Employer and Employee Strategies.

	Employer argues:	*Employee argues:*
Company at fault	The case belongs within workers' compensation system (a work-related injury).	The case falls outside the system (not a work-related injury).
Company not at fault	The case falls outside the system.	The case belongs within the system.

recover a large personal injury damage award from the company. When your company is not at fault, you will argue that the case falls outside the system, in which case the company owes nothing. Employee arguments are opposite those that you make in the two scenarios.

Step Three: Develop Business Strategies and Solutions That Minimize Workers' Compensation Costs

Once you have exhausted the traditional response mechanisms of flight or fight, it is time to search for longer-range business strategies that minimize workers' compensation costs. Many businesses have already joined the search for these strategies, which fall into three categories: greater care in screening job applicants, collection and analysis of data relating to workplace injury, and return of employees to work as soon as possible. See Figure 3.1.

Exercise Care in Screening Job Applicants
Insurance industry experts estimate that 20 percent of workers' compensation claims are fraudulent.[23] Thus one goal of the screening process is to spot applicants who might submit fraudulent claims. Another goal is to identify applicants who have health problems that prevent them from performing the job. To achieve these goals, you should ask about medical conditions,

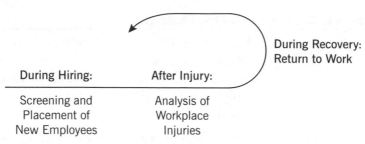

During Hiring:

Screening and
Placement of
New Employees

After Injury:

Analysis of
Workplace
Injuries

During Recovery:
Return to Work

Figure 3.1. Business Solutions to Workers' Compensation.

including injuries for which the applicant received workers' compensation. Under the Americans with Disabilities Act, these questions can only be asked after you have given the applicant a conditional job offer. Once this offer is made, you can also conduct a workers' compensation background check. Most states will provide you with this background information. You can cancel the conditional job offer in cases where the applicant has given you false information, the applicant cannot perform the job because of medical problems, or the applicant is a health or safety threat.[24]

Collect and Analyze Workers' Compensation Data
Workplace injury data can be analyzed through the use of a fairly sophisticated process called analysis of key factors. This process first identifies possible immediate causes of workplace injuries as well as "near misses." Once immediate causes have been identified, the focus then turns to underlying causes and problems. For example, if the immediate cause of an accident is a hole in a drill press (as in the "two finger" case discussed earlier in this chapter), why wasn't the defect identified before the worker began to use the machine?[25]

After completing your analysis, you must act promptly to correct immediate and underlying causes—or risk an intentional injury claim that will take future cases outside the workers' compensation system. On one level, this can be as simple as covering a dangerous hole in a machine. To encourage managers to take corrective action, one company produces an annual public report that describes injuries at specific sites and actions taken to improve safety. For example, a recent report notes, "In January an operator slipped off a staircase and injured his back. As a result, he was absent from work for a week. All stairs have meanwhile been coated with an anti-slip paint." Through this focus on safety, the company reduced its lost-workday cases from 560 in 1987 to 53 in 1996.[26]

On a more general level, an injury might be symptomatic of a general process that needs improvement or an entire class of problems that endanger a broad spectrum of workers. Addressing those problems often pays significant dividends. For example, repetitive stress injuries (sometimes called cumulative trauma) have been called "the first white collar mass tort."[27] These are skeletal or muscular injuries that result from repeated motion—for example, carpal tunnel syndrome, an injury that may result from repetitious work such as typing at a computer keyboard. It is estimated that repetitive stress injuries account for 56 percent of all workplace injuries and cost employers billions of dollars per year in workers' compensation.[28] Through ergonomics, also called human engineering, the workplace can be redesigned to reduce the number of injuries.

However, "less than a quarter of employers have an ergonomics program in place."[29] Companies often view workplace redesign with suspicion because of concerns about cost and effectiveness. Consequently, when faced with a new government regulation or a lawsuit, they tend to revert to the "fight" response. For instance, when the government cited a Firestone plant for twenty-three ergonomic violations, Firestone fought back, arguing that the government did not show the existence of ergonomic factors that were likely to cause death or serious physical harm.

Though the court in this instance sided with Firestone,[30] a focus on winning in court should not overshadow opportunities to reduce the costs of workplace injuries through redesign. For example, a plant manager in a sequin factory in New York reluctantly purchased adjustable chairs for employees and redesigned company equipment. As a result, annual repetitive stress injuries dropped from eighteen to five (in a workforce of four hundred) and workers' compensation costs dropped over a two-year period from $97,000 to $4,500.[31]

Return Employees to Work

A lingering workplace injury often creates suspicion and hostility between employers and employees. The employer might think that employees who remain at home for a long time are lazy and shirking work responsibilities. In some cases, a manager might even be relieved when a mediocre performer is slow in returning to work. According to the president of a janitorial services firm, "Some employers will say, 'good, there's a human resource problem I don't have to deal with. . . .' What the employer does by using the system to exile them to never-never land is subsidize their retirement."[32]

Meanwhile, an employee might think that an employer who does not remain in touch no longer cares about the employee's welfare. A physician who runs a clinic for injured workers observed that "At home, workers sit around, gain weight, lose tone, and they have all the psychological baggage that comes with being unproductive."[33] The situation may become legally risky if the injured worker begins to watch late-night television, where advertising by lawyers encourages legal action against employers for workplace injuries.

The solution is a program that includes constant communication between employers and injured workers along with attempts to return employees to work (even temporary jobs) as soon as possible. The janitorial services firm president contrasts this approach with the tactic of fighting for law reform: "Most executives still think they have to lobby through the legislature to get any relief. We've learned that you shouldn't wait for a change in the laws to help you. You have to take a hands-on approach and learn how to manage the workers' compensation system."[34]

Other Business Solutions to the Legal Problem
Beyond specific responses to workers' compensation costs, research indicates that general management style plays an important role in reducing workplace injury. This includes a commitment to improve business operations, using well-identified processes for hiring and advancing employees, providing regular feedback to employees, and treating employees with respect, empathy, and fairness.[35]

Step Four: Climb to the Balcony—Reframe Workers' Compensation Legal Issues as Business Opportunities

You are concerned that spiraling workers' compensation costs are affecting your ability to compete. You understand the nature of the legal problem (Step One). You consider moving your business to another state (flight) or decide to stand and fight both for a better system and for victory in individual cases (Step Two). You then search for business solutions to workers' compensation costs, such as greater care in screening job applicants, analysis of workplace injury data, and speedy return of employees to work (Step Three).

You are now ready to climb to the balcony and ask whether, in your intense focus on the legal aspects of workers' compensation, you are overlooking a big-picture business concern that might create an opportunity for competitive advantage. In this case, the view from the balcony should reveal that your key business concern is the impact that injured employees have on your business, an impact that is far greater than workers' compensation costs. When employees are injured, production is delayed and you must bring in replacements, who have to be trained. These indirect costs range from two to ten times your direct workers' compensation costs and might eventually result in layoffs, delayed expansion, and pressure to raise the price of your product.[36]

Viewed from a total cost perspective, the business solutions designed to reduce legal costs suddenly appear inadequate. Why? Because these solutions are all directed toward workplace injuries. Reducing workplace injuries is necessary but not sufficient to gain competitive advantage for the simple reason that many—probably most—injuries *do not occur on the job.* And these off-the-job injuries are just as likely to delay production and create the need for replacement workers as injuries at work.

Once you have gained the "balcony" perspective of the business concern, your response should be clear. Instead of focusing on workplace injuries, you should integrate the management of workplace and off-the-job injuries. This integration takes two forms: injury prevention both on and off the job and combined administration of workers' compensation and disability benefits.

Injury Prevention at Home and at Work
Many companies are on the path toward injury prevention with on-site "wellness" programs, often complete with company fitness centers where safe forms of exercise are emphasized. According to a study of Xerox employees published in 2001 in the *Journal of Occupational and Environmental Medicine,* a reduction in injuries resulted in a 5:1 return on the company's investment in a wellness program.[37] Beyond injury prevention, these programs are useful in the recruitment and retention of employees. And improved health is also likely to improve employee productivity. According to a study published by the President's Council on Physical Fitness and Sports, fitness programs save between $1.15 and $5.52 for each dollar spent.[38]

But an integrated approach to injuries should not stop with fitness programs. Off-the-job injuries should receive the same scrutiny and analysis as workplace injuries. Biking, skating, skiing, shoveling snow, and canoeing are among the myriad activities that threaten greater injury (and greater financial consequences to your company) than workplace dangers. For this reason, a refinery manager at Tate and Lyle notes that the company promotes safety at home as well as at work: "We mail employee notices about common sense issues, such as wearing the proper personal protective equipment or how to mow your lawn safely. We even sent a carbon monoxide monitor to each employee's home."[39]

DuPont encourages employees who are injured at home to share details of their off-work injuries with supervisors so that the company can pass this information on to others in the company to encourage injury prevention. By encouraging "employees to take safety practices home with them," DuPont was able, over a ten-year period, to cut the number of off-the-job injuries by 66 percent. The benefits of this program extend beyond DuPont employees. When the husband of a DuPont consultant began to clean out a car trunk, she asked him to put on safety glasses. She reported, "A bungee cord wrapped around a tool chest let go and a hook smashed right into one of the safety glass lenses." The lens saved his eye.[40]

Integrated Benefits Administration

The second form of integration relates to administration of benefits. Historically, companies have administered two systems side by side, one focused on workers' compensation for workplace injuries and the other focused on disability insurance for other injuries. This dual system causes inefficiencies that are costly to your company. With an integrated system, the same administrator will handle the claim regardless of where the injury occurred.[41]

An integrated system also promotes a uniform approach to claims analysis and return-to-work programs. For instance, the administrator of a company's disability program may be more lax in attempting to return employees to work than the administrator of the workers' compensation program. A furniture manufacturer says, "We all knew intuitively we were saving money by getting people back to work early. But we've also improved processes and totally realigned our culture around a return-to-work focus, regardless of where disability occurs. It's also easier for our employees to understand the new system, and their productivity has improved dramatically."[42]

Other benefits of an integrated system are summarized in Exhibit 3.2. An insurance company that offers an integrated system to employers reported that in the first three months of operation, their total costs and the duration of short-term disabilities both dropped 10 percent, attorney involvement (which often results when employees are confused about dual processes) dropped almost 50 percent, and "double dipping" from dual plans was eliminated.[43]

Beyond integration, one company's climb to the balcony resulted in consulting opportunities relating to workers' compensation. DuPont has long been recognized as a leader in workplace safety. DuPont's focus on safety originated in the nineteenth century, when the company manufactured gunpowder and employees suffered injury as a result of frequent explosions. In fact, DuPont's factory buildings blew up so often that the company

Exhibit 3.2. Benefits of an Integrated System.

Single contact point for all claims.

Consistent case management for all injuries (for example, return to work program).

Immediate intervention on behalf of all disabled employees, regardless of where injury occurred.

Streamlined claims investigation.

Consolidated reporting that allows indentification of trends.

Source: Lane and Lichman, "Making 24 Hour Coverage Work," *Risk Management,* November 1998. Used by permission of Risk Management Society Publishing.

redesigned them with stone walls on three sides and a wooden wall on the fourth, which faced the Brandywine Creek. With this design, an explosion would blow out only the wooden wall, which could be easily replaced. If you arrived at work in those days and someone told you that "Betty Sue went across the creek last night," that was a polite way of saying that Betty Sue had died in an explosion.[44]

It was once estimated that DuPont's emphasis on safety saved the company (when compared with a company with an average safety record) the equivalent of $500 million in sales. Figure 3.2 illustrates the relationship between shareholder value, sales volume, and DuPont's safety goals. Based on its success with safety programs over the years, DuPont has developed a global consulting practice that provides safety advice and resources to other companies.

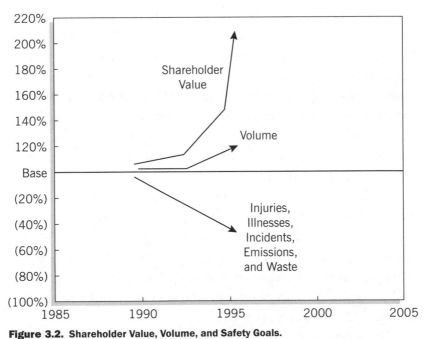

Figure 3.2. Shareholder Value, Volume, and Safety Goals.
Source: Executive Safety News (1997). Available online: http://www.dupont.com/safety/esn97–1/botline.html. Used by permission of DuPont Safety Resources.

■ Apply the Manager's Legal Plan to Wrongful Discharge

Wrongful discharge cases are especially common. One survey revealed that 55 percent of the companies surveyed had been sued by an employee over a recent twelve-month period, and wrongful discharge was one of the two most frequent claims asserted in these cases.[45] The other frequent claim was based on gender discrimination or sexual harassment, taken up later in this chapter. In another survey, almost two out of three executives indicated that employees had sued them or had threatened suit on similar grounds in a one-year period.[46] The following sections show how the Manager's Legal Plan applies to wrongful discharge litigation.

Step One: Understand Wrongful Discharge Law

As a starting point you should be familiar with the basic concepts of law relating to wrongful discharge. The fundamental legal principle that governs wrongful discharge in the United States is the employment-at-will rule. Under this rule, you can hire and fire employees at will in all states but Montana (which requires good cause for dismissals). This rule does not apply to employees governed by union collective bargaining agreements, but the overwhelming majority of employees in private industry do not belong to unions.

Most other countries do not follow an employment-at-will rule. Instead, the typical approach is that employers must provide advance notice when employees are discharged and also must compensate employees who are fired without cause. For example, an average forty-five-year-old employee in Italy who had worked for a company for twenty years would be entitled to over $125,000 in compensation.[47]

In recent years, U.S. law has moved closer to the law in other countries as courts have developed three exceptions to the employment-at-will rule. First, the rule does not apply if the company has made statements to employees or in company documents that create contractual rights that override the rule. For instance, during negotiations with a company, a person who was later hired as director of marketing was told by a company officer that "if you are doing the job, you can be assured that you will not be discharged." When he was later discharged for no apparent reason, he sued the company—claiming that this oral statement prevented the company from firing him without cause. He recovered $300,000.[48]

Second, a company must act in good faith in dismissing employees. In one case, a company fired a salesperson who had worked for the company for twenty-five years. A jury decided that the termination, which took place the next business day after the salesperson had obtained a $5 million order, resulted from the company's desire to reduce the employee's bonus that would have been due as a result of the sale. An appellate court noted that the employee's contract was "a classic terminable at will employment contract . . . [that] reserved to the parties an explicit power to terminate the contract without cause." But the court affirmed the jury decision because a company's decision to fire an employee must be made in good faith.[49]

Third, a dismissal may not violate public policy. For example, a nurse was hired as an at-will employee by a hospital. She went on a camping trip with her supervisor and employees of other hospitals. During the trip, members of the group staged a parody of the song "Moon River," which allegedly included their mooning the audience. The nurse refused to participate in this parody and in other activities that made her feel uncomfortable. Before the trip the nurse had received favorable performance evaluations. Shortly after the trip, she was terminated.

When the lower courts dismissed her lawsuit, the case was appealed to the Supreme Court of Arizona. The court held that "an employer may fire for good cause or for no cause. He may not fire for bad cause—that which violates public policy." Does refusal to participate in mooning violate public policy? The supreme court justices admitted, "We have little expertise in the techniques of mooning." But, citing the state indecent exposure law, the court concluded that "termination of employment for refusal to participate in public exposure of one's buttocks is a termination contrary to the policy of this state."[50]

In addition to these three exceptions, it is not unusual for an employee to allege defamation in connection with the discharge. For example, in one case an insurance salesperson named Larry was fired by his employer. When he was unable to find employment with other firms, he hired an investigator. Posing as a prospective employer, the investigator contacted the office manager of the firm where Larry had worked. The office manager told the investigator that Larry was "irrational, ruthless, and disliked by office personnel . . . a classical sociopath . . . a zero, a Jekyll and Hyde person who was lacking . . . scruples." Because the statements were untrue, this conversation cost the employer $1.9 million in damages when Larry filed suit for defamation.[51] It is estimated that one-third of all defamation cases are brought by fired employees against their former managers.[52]

The combination of the exceptions to the employment-at-will rule and defamation law has produced a judicial lottery where some employees win large damage awards and many win nothing. California is notorious for large awards in wrongful discharge cases. A few years ago, when I was a visiting professor at Stanford University, an article in the local paper told the story of a Silicon Valley employee, David, who was fired by an electronics firm. According to the article, the firm replaced David, a top salesperson, with someone who had financial ties to the person who fired him. The company investigated the matter, but then claimed that the file was lost. When David sued the company for wrongful discharge, he also claimed that the company distributed defamatory information about him. Based on this combination of factors, the jury awarded David $61 million in damages. The article indicated that the company planned an appeal.[53]

Large awards are not confined to California. A jury in Kentucky awarded two former Ashland Oil employees $70 million after the company wrongfully discharged them when they protested illegal foreign payments. The case was eventually settled for "only" $25 million.[54] And a Texas jury awarded a former energy company employee $124 million for a wrongful discharge after the employee refused to prepare documents that contained misleading information. The Texas case was also eventually settled for an estimated $25 million.[55]

Step Two: React to the Wrongful Discharge Legal Problem Through Flight or Fight

Flight from wrongful discharge litigation is difficult. Although several states have not adopted all three exceptions to the employment-at-will rule—and a few (such as Georgia) have adopted none of them—legal trends indicate that these exceptions will eventually arrive in everyone's neighborhood. Flight outside the United States is not realistic because, as noted, most countries provide automatic compensation when there is no cause for dismissal. Unlike the judicial lottery in the United States, the laws in other countries make most discharged employees winners, even though the amounts might not be as large as in the United States.

The wrongful discharge fight includes two possible options. One option is to play the lottery by fighting individual claims. With this strategy, you may win most cases. As an attorney with the ACLU has noted: "The average employee who has been wrongfully terminated has as much chance of getting a jury trial as sprouting wings and flying to the moon."[56] But you also risk an occasional large damage award similar to those awarded by juries in California, Kentucky, and Texas.

Another option is to fight for law reform. This fight occurs on two fronts. First, approximately half the states have enacted laws that protect employers from liability for defamation. For example, these laws commonly create a presumption that a former employer who provides information to a prospective employer is acting in good faith. But this protection does not apply when the former employer knows that the information is false. Depending on state law, the former employer also may not be protected when providing information that is not related to job performance (such as lifestyle information) or when providing a reference that was not requested by a prospective employer.[57]

The second law reform fight represents an attack on the employment-at-will rule. For example, a model act has been drafted that would operate much like workers' compensation in that an employee gives up the right to bring suit for wrongful discharge and, in return, is entitled to reinstatement with back pay or to an award of up to three years' salary, which would be determined by an arbitrator. Employers view this type of reform differently, depending on whether they are in states that have adopted the exceptions to the employment-at-will rule. In states where the exceptions apply, employers may be subject to large damage awards and would welcome a law that limits damages. According to one attorney: "Employers in California might welcome this legislation while employers in Georgia will laugh at it."[58] To date, only Montana has adopted legislation that eliminates the traditional employment-at-will rule.

Step Three: Develop Business Strategies and Solutions That Prevent Wrongful Discharge Liability

Given the high financial risks associated with wrongful discharge litigation, most companies have taken a number of measures to minimize liability. Consider especially three types of approaches for preventing potential liability.

Review Your Hiring Practices

First, review your hiring practices. Careful screening of prospective employees to eliminate those who are candidates for dismissal down the road is an obvious approach. Unfortunately, given the defamation risks associated with comments about an employee's performance, information is difficult to obtain from former employers.

Another hiring strategy is to increase the number of temporary employees. Companies have long used this strategy outside the United States, where the costs of dismissal are high because employees discharged without cause receive automatic compensation. For instance, a few years ago I helped open a University of Michigan center in Paris. Before interviewing potential staff members, I received careful instruction from a French lawyer on the importance of hiring the staff on a short-term contract. At the end of the contract, she explained, the University could decide whether to renew or terminate the contract, without the costs that would be associated with dismissing a regular employee. It is estimated that close to 90 percent of new hires in France are hired under this form of contract.[59] In the United States, temporary workers, informally called "permatemps," have become permanent fixtures at many companies.[60]

Document Review and Training

A second strategy is directed toward statements that might create an exception to the employment-at-will rule. Train and constantly remind managers that statements to staff like "as long as you do a good job, you'll have a job" create an inappropriate expectation that the company will fire employees only when there is good cause.

Also review company documents and delete language that might overturn the employment-at-will rule. For example, a few years ago I gave a presentation at a major utility company in Texas. In preparing the talk, I reviewed the company's recruiting brochure in the University of Michigan career development office. A statement in the brochure caught my eye. To paraphrase, it read: "After joining the company, you will first participate in an orientation program. You then will be assigned to a permanent position that is consistent with your career goals." The problem here is "permanent," a word that should be permanently avoided in all company documents. During my presentation I quoted the brochure. Immediately afterward, two human resource managers mentioned their concern about this language and asked for a copy of the brochure.

The following year the company invited me back for another presentation. Once again, I visited the career development office to review the recruiting brochure. I noticed that the company had a new brochure and, when I turned to the page with the quoted statement, discovered that the language had been "slightly" altered. Paraphrasing again, it now read: "At the end of the orientation program, an interesting career *may* be waiting for you" (my emphasis). Clearly the company had understood the problem with the original brochure!

The third strategy is to attempt to reduce liability for defamatory statements by instructing your staff that they should not comment on the job performance of former employees. In fact, they should make no comments at all but should, instead, forward all inquiries to human resources. A human resources professional will then provide very limited information regarding the time of employment and title but will not discuss performance matters. This approach obviously causes problems for prospective employers trying to investigate someone's employment history. It also causes problems when you have dismissed someone for reasons unrelated to performance (for example, when you downsize your business) and want to say something positive to a prospective employer. Nevertheless, in a survey of Fortune 500 firms, all respondents said that they do not provide references.[61]

Step Four: Climb to the Balcony—Reframe Wrongful Discharge Legal Issues as Business Opportunities

If I play a word association game with a manager and say "wrongful discharge," the most likely response is "high damage award." The fear of a headline damage award of the type rendered by juries in California, Texas, Kentucky, and other states has caused managers to focus on the business solutions just described.

Problems with the Conventional Focus
There are two problems with this focus. The first is that in some cases conventional approaches are flawed. As one example, take the "no comment" approach to requests for information from prospective employers. This approach is fine as far as it goes, but it overlooks the fact that your conversations are not only with outsiders. For instance, what do you say when one of your staff asks you why Larry is no longer with the company? A "no comment" response is likely to cause morale problems and unrest among your employees. But a comment that is untrue opens the door to a defamation lawsuit. For example, an employee who had worked for a company for forty-one years was fired after the company accused him of stealing a $35 company telephone. The employee, who claimed that the telephone belonged to him, sued the company for defamation after it posted notices on company bulletin boards accusing him of theft. A jury awarded the employee $15.5 million in damages and the case was later settled.[62]

What if you say nothing to outsiders or other employees? Might there still be liability for defamation? Yes, said an Illinois federal court in a case brought by a trader on the Chicago Board of Trade who had worked for a brokerage firm for twelve years. The broker alleged that one afternoon three of the firm's officials unexpectedly went to his office and, in plain view of other employees, interrogated him about his expense reports. They then escorted him from the office without allowing him to speak to his staff or take his belongings. He alleged that other brokerage firms would not discharge a high-level employee in this manner unless there had been a violation of the criminal law or a breach of ethics. When the firm asked the court to dismiss the case, the judge denied the request.[63]

Still another flaw with the "no comment" approach is the risk of liability for what you say to the discharged employee, even if no one else is present. For example, let's assume that you fire one of your employees, Frank, and you advise him privately that the reason for the discharge is that he is a sociopath, which is not true. Frank then applies for a job with another company. A manager from the company calls you and asks why Frank was fired. You refuse to comment, as required by company policy. The manager then asks Frank to explain why he left the company. Frank's choice is to lie about the reasons you gave, which is not an attractive alternative, or to explain that you told him that the reason for the discharge is that he is a sociopath.

After hearing Frank's explanation the manager (understandably) decides not to hire Frank. Frank then sues you for defamation. "Wait a minute," you say. "I did not defame Frank. He defamed himself by passing on the information." This is still defamation, according to courts in several states, because Frank had no choice. He was compelled to defame himself.

In one "compelled self-defamation" case, four insurance company employees were terminated for what the company called "gross insubordination." The company policy was to provide prospective employers with only dates of employment and the final job titles of former employees. When these employees told prospective employers the reasons they were given for the discharge, they had difficulty finding jobs. The Supreme Court of Minnesota upheld a large damage award to the employees.[64] In summary, the conventional "no comment" approach is flawed because it overlooks conversations with internal staff, actions that might be defamatory, and comments made privately to an employee.

A second problem with conventional business strategies is that they address a symptom (a potentially large damage award) of a deeper problem. This deeper problem should be revealed when you remove yourself from the legal fray and climb to the balcony to gain perspective. Once on the balcony you should ask yourself: What is the real cost of wrongful discharge litigation? Is it the potential damage award or is it the cost generated by the fear of litigation and damage awards? If the latter, what are these costs and how can they be addressed?

The Rand Corporation conducted an in-depth empirical study that assessed the impact of the erosion of the employment-at-will rule. The study concluded that the indirect costs of the exceptions to the employment-at-will rule are a hundred times greater than the direct legal costs (such as jury awards) that receive the most attention from managers. The indirect costs include keeping poor performers, making severance payments, and forcing managers to use complex and time-consuming processes before discharging anyone. In other words, the view from the balcony is that company costs in avoiding litigation far exceed actual litigation costs.[65]

Manage by Fact
Once you have reframed the legal concern (high litigation costs) as a business concern (the impact of keeping poor performers or giving them large severance packages), you should then reexamine your business solutions. One solution that should immediately come to mind is a key feature of any quality program: manage by fact. In other words, tell the truth.

Two aspects of truth-telling are especially important in the context of wrongful termination. First, telling the truth is critically important in the performance review process because your ability to show cause for dismissing a poor performer minimizes the exceptions to the employment-at-will rule. As an HR director at a large energy company once told me, "We are an at-will company, but we always try to show cause."

But this is easier said than done. If you are a typical manager, it is difficult to be completely candid and honest when you sit down with an employee to review performance. For example, one company rates employees on a scale of 1 to 10, with 10 as the highest rating. A study of the records at this company found that no supervisor gave employees a rating of lower than 8 and the average score was 9.[66] In an environment where managers are not candid and honest, even poor performers will walk into court with performance reviews that indicate that their work has been "great." The solution: Use candid, fact-based statements when you conduct performance reviews.

Second, truth-telling is important in conversations about the performance of former employees. Truth is a defense in a defamation action. As we have seen, the "no comment" approach that dominates business today is only partially effective because it focuses on external communications while liability may extend to comments made within the company. The "no comment" approach also makes it difficult for your company to obtain information from other companies about prospective employees. By contrast, a truth-telling approach will protect a company across the board—whether the communication is with prospective employers, other employees within the firm, or the discharged employee.

Beyond its impact in wrongful termination cases, truth-telling is important in establishing trust within your company. In a world of flat, lean organizations and new forms of business alliances, trust is essential to competitive advantage. As noted in an article in the *Economist*, "The arguments in favour of trust seem overwhelming. Trust reduces the costs and delays associated with traditional monitoring systems and formal legal contracts. It enables companies to engage the hearts and minds of their employees, not just their passive compliance."[67]

Replacing "no comment" policies with management by fact and truth-telling in your internal and external communication represents a major step toward creating an environment of trust.

Although wrongful discharge is a serious matter for both companies and their discharged employees, it is not devoid of humor. Exhibit 3.3 contains examples of quotations drawn from actual performance reviews. And Exhibit 3.4 contains some tongue-in-cheek recommendations for making truthful statements when writing reference letters for former employees who were poor performers.

Exhibit 3.3. Quotations from Performance Reviews.

"His men would follow him anywhere, but only out of morbid curiosity."

"Works well when under constant supervision and cornered like a rat in a trap."

"When she opens her mouth, it seems that this is only to change whichever foot was previously in there."

"He would be out of his depth in a parking lot puddle."

"He sets low personal standards, and then consistently fails to achieve them."

"This employee is depriving a village somewhere of an idiot."

Exhibit 3.4. Ambiguous Recommendations.

For someone who has engaged in criminal activity:
"He's a man of many convictions."
or
"I'm sorry we let her get away."

For someone who is untrustworthy:
"Her true ability is deceiving."

For someone who is unqualified:
"I most enthusiastically recommend this person with no qualifications whatsoever."

For someone who is lazy:
"In my opinion, you will be very fortunate to get this person to work for you."

Source: "Art of Lying," *Wall Street Journal,* March 22, 1994, p. 1, quoting Robert J. Thornton, *The Lexicon of Intentionally Ambiguous Recommendations (LIAR).*

■ Apply the Manager's Legal Plan to Sexual Harassment

As noted in the preceding section, a survey indicates that most companies have been sued in a recent twelve-month period and that a large proportion of these suits allege gender discrimination, sexual harassment, or both. It is estimated that up to 90 percent of women and 15 percent of men have been sexually harassed in the workplace.[68] Among the headline-grabbing jury verdicts or settlements in gender discrimination or sexual harassment cases are an $80.7 million jury award to a United Parcel Service manager (although she may be unable to collect the entire amount because of a cap on punitive damages under federal law),[69] a jury verdict that (with interest) will total over $45 million to a female millwright who worked at DaimlerChrysler,[70] a $34 million settlement that Mitsubishi agreed to pay approximately 350 female employees who worked at a plant in Normal, Illinois,[71] and a $17.5 million settlement (including the cost of a training program) resulting from sexual harassment at two Ford plants near Chicago.[72]

It may be comforting to some that lawyers and government are not immune from claims of sexual harassment. For instance, a jury ordered a law firm to pay $6.9 million in punitive damages to a legal secretary in a sexual harassment lawsuit, which was almost twice what she had requested.[73] The trial court judge later reduced the punitive award to $3.5 million, but also awarded the secretary $1.8 million in attorney fees.[74] And in early 2000, the federal government agreed to pay more than $508 million to 1,100 women who were subjected to discrimination by the U.S. Information Agency.[75]

What is not comforting is that individual managers may be sued along with their companies. These managers often face a double penalty when they are discharged and forced to pay damages as a result of misconduct. In a case decided in late 1999, for instance, a jury awarded $18.8 million (which the trial court reduced to $10.3 million) to a sales representative who alleged sexual harassment by her manager. The manager was fired and was also held liable for part of the award.[76] In the case involving the law firm, the lawyer who allegedly committed the harassment resigned after being told he would be removed from the firm—and he was also held liable for $225,000 in punitive damages.

Step One: Understand the Law of Sexual Harassment

Managers need a clear understanding of sexual harassment law. Federal law is grounded in the Civil Rights Act of 1964, which makes sex discrimination illegal. Sex discrimination includes sexual harassment, which was defined by the Supreme Court in 1986.[77] According to the Court, a key factor in determining whether conduct is lawful is whether it is welcome. Conduct that is welcome does not constitute harassment; unwelcome sexual conduct is harassment.

The Supreme Court further defined two types of unwelcome conduct (see Figure 3.3). One type is *quid pro quo* or "this for that" sexual harassment. "This" is an economic benefit that a manager might offer someone in exchange for "that," which is a sexual relationship. The classic example is the "casting couch." The movie director says to the young starlet, "Sleep with me and I'll make you a star."

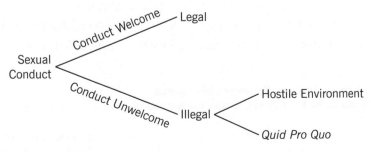

Figure 3.3. Sexual Harassment Law.

The second type of sexual harassment results when the work environment is hostile because of sexual misconduct. In defining "hostile environment" sexual harassment, the Supreme Court quoted guidelines developed by the Equal Employment Opportunity Commission. These guidelines provide that sexual misconduct constitutes prohibited sexual harassment when "such conduct has the purpose or effect of unreasonably interfering with an individual's work performance or creating an intimidating, hostile, or offensive working environment."[78]

Step Two: React to the Sexual Harassment Legal Problem Through Flight or Fight

Neither flight nor fight is effective in addressing sexual harassment. Flight is not realistic in a world where sexual harassment laws have become commonplace. Studies around the world indicate that women are subjected to or witness sexual harassment at work. Foreign legislatures have responded with laws that in some cases are more punitive than the U.S. law. In France, for instance, a supervisor who obtains sexual favors through abuse of authority faces up to one year in prison and a heavy fine.[79] Even in a conservative, predominantly Muslim country like Malaysia, a court has cited U.S. court decisions in deciding in favor of an employee who alleged sexual harassment.[80]

Fighting for sexual harassment law reform is equally unrealistic. This leaves the option of fighting individual cases when you feel that the charges are false. Although fighting false claims of sexual harassment is important, a court battle also creates the risk of a high damage award, as illustrated by the cases discussed earlier.

Step Three: Develop Business Strategies and Solutions That Prevent Sexual Harassment

This step is especially promising in the sexual harassment arena because the Supreme Court has provided companies with clear guidelines on how to minimize their liability for sexual harassment.

A 1998 Supreme Court decision involved a case brought by an ocean lifeguard who worked for the City of Boca Raton, Florida. She claimed that her two supervisors created a "sexually hostile atmosphere" by subjecting her and other female lifeguards to "uninvited and offensive touching," and that they made lewd remarks and spoke of women in offensive terms. The trial court found that one of the supervisors: "repeatedly touched the bodies of female employees without invitation, would put his arm around Faragher, with his hand on her buttocks, and once made contact with another female lifeguard in a motion of sexual stimulation. He made crudely demeaning references to women generally, and once commented disparagingly on Faragher's shape. During a job interview with a woman he hired as a lifeguard, Terry said that the female lifeguards had sex with their male counterparts and asked whether she would do the same."[81]

Based on these findings, the trial court held that Boca Raton was liable. The case eventually reached the Supreme Court. In upholding the trial court decision, the Court first noted that employers are liable when they take tangible action—for example, causing economic injury to an employee such as denial of a promotion or raise. Even when the employer does not take action, as in this case, an employer is liable unless it can prove two elements: "(a) that the employer exercised reasonable care to prevent and correct promptly any sexually harassing behavior, and (b) that the plaintiff employee unreasonably failed to take advantage of any preventive or corrective opportunities provided by the employer."[82]

The practical message from this language is that you should take three measures to prevent liability. First, adopt an antiharassment policy. Ideally, the policy will provide examples of the acts that are prohibited by the company. Here is an example of prohibited acts listed in one company's policy: "Repeated, offensive sexual flirtations, advances, propositions; continued or repeated verbal abuse of a sexual nature; graphic verbal commentaries about an individual's body; sexually degrading words used to describe an individual; display of sexually suggestive objects or pictures."[83]

Second, establish a complaint procedure that will result in prompt correction of any suspect behavior. This procedure should provide alternative avenues for complaint—for example, to a supervisor, or to human resources, or to a peer group. Both the anti-harassment policy and the complaint procedure should be communicated effectively to employees.

Third, provide sexual harassment training. Supervisors should have special training sessions that cover their unique responsibilities in responding to complaints. All employees should be made aware that men and women perceive actions and statements differently. For instance, how would you feel about being sexually propositioned in the workplace? A study cited by a Florida court found that around two-thirds of men would be flattered, while 15 percent would feel insulted. These proportions are reversed for women. As a result, the court decided that the test to determine whether a hostile environment exists depends on how a reasonable woman would view the workplace.[84] With this perspective, the Golden Rule gives way to a Platinum Rule: Do unto others as they would want done.

A company that takes these measures should be successful in defending a sexual harassment case. For example, in one case decided after the Supreme Court stated its guidelines, an employee was assigned to a new shift. One of her co-workers made comments (among others) "in front of other co-workers that if Fenton had any more children she would be wider than the Grand Canyon and that she would have to use shims off of one of the machines in the shop to make any man want her again; that he was going to call 1–900 numbers and 'play with himself', and that men 'only want one thing from you.'"[85]

The employee reported the comments to a supervisor, who the same day met with the plant superintendent. A report was immediately made to a human resources manager, who met with the complaining employee the next day. He investigated the matter and within four days the co-worker was reassigned to another area. The co-worker was also advised that if the comments continued he would be subject to disciplinary action. The court concluded that the employer was not liable because it took prompt corrective action.

Step Four: Climb to the Balcony—Reframe Sexual Harassment Legal Issues as Business Opportunities

The mention of sexual harassment brings to a manager's mind thoughts of litigation and large damage awards. There is also often a feeling that sexual harassment training is a necessary evil that pulls employees away from more productive work and is forced on companies by the legal system. As the president of a high-tech company told a partner in a leading law firm following the 1998 Supreme Court decisions, "I have to lay something out very bluntly. I have had very little use for lawyers. They cause more problems than they solve."[86]

But is sexual harassment a legal problem or a business problem? If there were no laws governing sexual misconduct, would it still make sense for businesses to follow the approaches that are currently mandated by law? When you climb to the balcony to move away from the legal fray and gain a broader perspective, a different picture might emerge. This perspective was best summarized by an executive vice president for a major power company: "[Sexual harassment] is a business issue. It doesn't have to do with law or morality but about having a productive work force."[87]

Your employees cannot be productive if they must worry about the abuse of power that sexual harassment represents. If, for instance, women make up half the workforce and over 50 percent of women experience sexual harassment on the job, one out of four of your employees must worry about something other than doing a good job. Companies that eliminate sexual harassment have the opportunity to seize competitive advantage by allowing their employees to focus on customer needs. As one expert on sexual harassment noted, "there's quite a consistent body of literature that shows that [with sexual harassment] work performance declines, and as a result quality of performance, and attendance. All of that ultimately has to hurt the company."[88]

From your perspective on the balcony, you should be able to see that the real issue is not compliance with the law of sexual harassment but, instead, removing barriers that prevent your employees from being as productive as possible. In effect, your sexual harassment policy should not be limited to "We will not tolerate sexual harassment." Instead, the spirit of the policy should be: "We will create a productive work environment that is market-driven and customer focused."

With this perspective, your horizon broadens to elimination of barriers beyond sexual harassment (which to date has received most of the media attention—possibly because it is a sexier topic). According to one employment law expert, many companies "broadcast their sexual-harassment policies, but they have nothing in them about any other kind of harassment."[89] Yet the Equal Employment Opportunity Commission and various courts have concluded that the Supreme Court guidelines apply to other types of harassment covered by the Civil Rights Act, such as race and religion.

For example, an African American employee brought suit against Budget Rent-A-Car alleging racial discrimination. A federal court denied Budget's motion to dismiss the case, noting that the employee's claims, if proven, could result in a finding of racial harassment. The employee alleged that his supervisor treated him more harshly than other employees and used racial epithets. This is testimony from another employee:

> I was in his [the supervisor's] office one morning and he was looking out the window and pointed to the black service agents and remarked how lazy they were and how slow they worked

and said that was typical of blacks. At that point he made a comparison about some Vietnamese workers I had and said that they were much better workers and that he wished he could get rid of the "niggers" and hire some more Vietnamese workers. . . . [He] said that he wanted to get Anthony to quit because it would be difficult to fire him because he was black.[90]

The court noted that, under the 1998 Supreme Court guidelines, Budget did not offer proof that its harassment policy was distributed to employees or that it offered racial harassment training to its managers. Budget also did not prove that it promptly corrected complaints of racial harassment.

With a broader perspective that focuses on productivity, it is easier for all employees to understand that harassment is not limited to the acts of managers and other employees; the company also has a duty to prevent discriminatory conduct by customers. For instance, a waitress sued the Pizza Hut franchise where she worked claiming hostile environment sexual harassment. Two "crude and rowdy" male customers had eaten at the restaurant several times and had made sexually offensive remarks to the waitress, such as "I would like to get into your pants." One evening, when no one on the wait staff wanted to serve these customers, the shift manager ordered the waitress to serve them. One of the customers said "that she smelled good and asked what kind of cologne she was wearing." When she told the customer that it was "none of his business," he grabbed her by the hair. When she told the manager what happened, and that she did not want to wait on them, he responded: "You wait on them. You were hired to be a waitress. You waitress." When she delivered a pitcher of beer to the customers, one of them "pulled her by the hair, grabbed her breast, and put his mouth on her breast."[91]

The waitress then told the manager that she was quitting and called her husband, who picked her up. At trial, an expert witness testified that the waitress, who had been sexually assaulted by a friend of her father while a teenager, "exhibited classic symptoms of post-traumatic stress disorder and major depression." The jury awarded her $200,000 in damages plus over $38,000 in attorney fees and costs. In upholding the verdict, an appellate court concluded that an employer should be held liable regardless of whether a hostile environment is created by "a co-employee or a nonemployee, since the employer ultimately controls the conditions of the work environment."[92]

Cases involving racial or religious discrimination or harassment by customers violate the law. But what if certain forms of discrimination or harassment do not violate the law? For example, discrimination on the basis of sexual orientation is not prohibited by federal law, nor by the law of most states. Yet this form of discrimination has the same impact on workplace morale and productivity as discrimination based on race, sex, or religion. A Dow Chemical Company booklet entitled "Respect and Responsibility" goes to the heart of the matter:

> When an individual experiences harassment, the cost may be felt emotionally. Work team environments may become strained and staff morale may be lowered. Dow may suffer absenteeism, employee turnover, increased accidents, reduced productivity, and decreased quality—not to mention the legal ramifications of such actions. . . . In addition to unlawful harassment, Dow's Harassment Policy prohibits harassment in any form. When people feel they are being mistreated, it can have a measurable impact on our ability to do business. . . . Harassment typically falls into one of two categories: hostile work environment and quid pro quo. However it should be clear that Dow will not tolerate harassment in any form—[whether aimed at] a person's weight, height, sexual orientation, etc. Bottom line, we want and expect an environment free from harassment for all Dow people.[93]

CHAPTER SUMMARY

This chapter has applied the Manager's Legal Plan to three legal concerns that dominate the employment relationship: workers' compensation, wrongful discharge, and sexual harassment.

Over the years, workers' compensation has been a major concern for business. Companies that control their workers' compensation costs have a significant opportunity to seize competitive advantage. The four-step Manager's Legal Plan reveals cost-reduction opportunities:

Step One. Understand the basic "give and take" of the system. It is designed to provide your employees with an exclusive remedy.

Step Two. Determine your legal response to the legal problem of workers' compensation. Your fundamental choices are flight (to a state with lower workers' compensation costs) or fight (for law reform or for victory on a case-by-case basis).

Step Three. Adopt business measures that address the legal problem. These fall into three categories: screening job applicants, analysis of workplace data, and return-to-work programs.

Step Four. Climb to the balcony for a big-picture perspective that reveals underlying business problems—notably production delays and the use of replacement workers—that are far more costly than workers' compensation legal costs. By focusing on these business problems, you can expand your safety initiatives beyond the workplace and integrate workers' compensation and disability systems in a manner that provides opportunities for competitive advantage.

Changes in the employment-at-will rule have created the potential for large damage awards against your company. Use the Manager's Legal Plan as follows:

Step One. Understand the nature of these changes, especially the three exceptions to the rule.

Step Two. Fight individual cases or fight for law reform.

Step Three. Adopt business strategies and solutions that are designed to prevent wrongful discharge litigation. These include greater use of temporary employees and careful review of company documents to ensure that they do not override the employment-at-will rule.

Step Four. Climb to the balcony, which will reveal business problems that are far more costly than the legal problem of expensive litigation, such as retention of poor performers and expensive severance packages. When the legal concern is reframed as a business problem, the dominant solution is to emphasize management by fact in the performance review process and in commenting on discharged employees. Management by fact, in turn, creates an environment of trust, which is important in gaining competitive advantage.

Sexual harassment allegations are common and costly to both individual managers and their employers. Use the Manager's Legal Plan as follows:

Step One. Understand the fundamental distinctions between welcome and unwelcome conduct, and between quid pro quo and hostile environment sexual harassment.
Step Two. Realize that traditional flight-or-fight responses are extremely limited in this area of the law.
Step Three. Develop business strategies in response to the legal problem of sexual harassment. These strategies include employee training and clear communication of your sexual harassment policy and complaint procedures.
Step Four. Use your perspective from the balcony to reframe the legal problem of sexual harassment as an opportunity for competitive advantage that focuses on the morale and productivity of your employees. With this perspective, the emphasis shifts to eliminating all forms of discrimination in the workplace, regardless of whether the law requires you to do so.

Questions to Consider

1. Have you developed strategies for minimizing workers' compensation costs, such as careful screening of job applicants and analysis of workers' compensation data?
2. Have you integrated the management of workplace and off-the-job injuries?

3. Have you developed strategies for minimizing wrongful discharge liability, including the use of temporary employees, document review, and training programs?
4. In light of the dangers in "no comment" policies regarding employee performance, do you emphasize management by fact?
5. Have you taken steps to eliminate all forms of discrimination at your company, even when not required to do so by law?

Use Regulation as a Source of Competitive Advantage

Transforming Environmental Regulation into Value Creation

Three groups of stakeholders are especially important to the success of your company and your ability to create value for your shareholders. Chapters Two and Three focused on two of these groups—customers and employees—and explored several of the most contentious issues in business today: product liability, workers' compensation, wrongful discharge, and sexual harassment. The third key stakeholder, government, represents the interests of society at large when it imposes rules and regulations on business. This chapter examines environmental protection to show that even governmental regulation can create opportunities for competitive advantage.

■ The Impact of Environmental Regulation

Protection of the environment is an especially controversial and costly form of regulation. You wear two hats when the government regulates your company to protect the environment. One is the hat of a citizen concerned with degradation of the environment. We are all aware of general scientific studies that highlight threats to the environment.[1]

A specific example of the impact that business has on the environment is provided by James Womack and Daniel Jones in their book, *Lean Thinking*.[2] A teenager in England pops open a can of cola, which takes a few minutes to drink, and then throws away the can. This simple act of consumption was preceded by many weeks of energy and other resource consumption in Australia, Norway, and England as bauxite ore was transformed into an aluminum can through purification, smelting, rolling mills, forming, painting, lacquering, and coating. The can was filled with a combination of elements that include sugar from beets raised in France, phosphorous from open pit mines in Idaho, and caffeine from a chemical manufacturer. Once filled, the cans were placed in cardboard cartons made of wood pulp from forests ranging from Siberia to British Columbia.[3]

Millions of production and transportation processes similar to the manufacture of a can of cola have a cumulative impact on the environment that affects both the natural and social systems on which business depends. As noted by one CEO, in referring to corporate social responsibility, "A healthy branch [business] cannot survive on a rotten trunk."[4]

Wearing your concerned citizen's hat, protection of the environment makes sense. But wearing your other hat, as a manager attempting to create shareholder value, you see environmental issues from a different perspective as you attempt to cope with a flood of environmental regulations. Over a trillion dollars has been spent on environmental compliance over the past twenty-five years, as the number of environmental rules and regulations at the local, state and federal levels has swelled from two thousand in 1970 to over a hundred thousand today. In Los Angeles, for instance, environmental protection rests with seventy-two different authorities.[5] It is no wonder that environmental concerns dominate discussion of legal matters in company annual reports.

Environmental regulation raises serious doubts about whether government bureaucrats use common sense in writing and enforcing rules. Philip Howard, in his best-selling book *The Death of Common Sense,* mentions a thirty-five page Environmental Protection Agency (EPA) rule that required companies to install equipment that would filter benzene in waste pipes. Amoco complied with the rule at a cost of $31 million, but also pointed out to the EPA that the benzene pollution in the waste pipes was insignificant. When EPA officials visited the Amoco work site, they realized that a simple, inexpensive solution was possible. The rule was, to use Howard's words, "almost perfect in its failure. It maximized the cost to Amoco while minimizing the benefit to the public."[6]

■ Apply the Manager's Legal Plan to Environmental Regulation

Given the scope of environmental regulation and the occasional lack of common sense in the creation and enforcement of specific rules, it may be tempting to focus your energy on fighting for saner rules or on minimizing the costs of compliance. While these measures may be necessary, they are not sufficient for you to gain advantage over your competitors. The four steps of the Manager's Legal Plan will help clarify opportunities for value creation that arise when environmental regulation is viewed as more than a cost of doing business.

**Step One: Understand the Legal
Framework of Environmental Regulation**

The first step in the Manager's Legal Plan is to understand the fundamental legal structure of environmental regulation.[7] Although this area of the law is complex, technical, and laden with more acronyms (like NAAQS, NPDES, CERCLA, and RCRA) than you may ever care to master, keeping the big picture in mind when you deal with specific environmental matters should help you seize competitive advantage. While the following road map of environmental law focuses on federal environmental protection, states also have their own environmental laws that parallel or complement federal law.

*National Environmental Policy and
the Environmental Protection Agency*

Environmental law is very old, with origins going back at least to medieval England, where laws established the seasons when soft coal could be burned. But a comprehensive set of U.S. environmental laws did not emerge until the last third of the twentieth century, when people began to recognize the threat to the environment. The year 1970 brought two landmark events, the signing into law of the National Environmental Policy Act (NEPA) and the creation of the Environmental Protection Agency (EPA).

NEPA declares that it is U.S. policy "to create and maintain conditions under which man and nature can exist in productive harmony, and fulfill the social, economic, and other requirements of present and future generations of Americans." One tool for accomplishing this goal is a requirement that federal agencies must prepare an environmental impact statement (EIS) in every recommendation for legislation and whenever engaged in a major federal action that significantly impacts environmental quality. The EIS provides an assessment of likely environmental impacts of alternative courses of action.

While NEPA articulates national policy, the act applies only to activities of federal agencies. The EPA has a greater direct impact on business. This agency assists the government and private business in halting environmental deterioration, creates environmental regulations, and monitors industry for violation of federal law. The EPA has a variety of enforcement options, ranging from informal responses (such as a warning letter) to referral to the Department of Justice for criminal prosecution. While the EPA carries out its mission through approximately three dozen federal laws, a dozen of these laws (the "clean dozen") that are especially important fall within five categories, as described in the following sections. See Figure 4.1.

Water Pollution
Although legislation governing U.S. waterways goes back to the late 1800s, the centerpiece of water pollution laws is the Clean Water Act. This act is designed to restore the "chemical, physical, and biological integrity of the Nation's waters." The act requires states to set water quality standards for various uses of water (such as drinking, recreation, and fishing), controls municipal sewage systems, and authorizes the EPA to protect marshes and other wetlands. The act also establishes strict standards for private industry's discharge of pollutants into waterways and sewage systems. Under the National Pollutant Discharge Elimination System (NPDES), you must obtain a permit if you want to discharge pollutants from a "point source" (for example, a pipe). Disposal of materials into the ocean requires an EPA permit under a separate law.

A second notable law relating to water quality is the Safe Drinking Water Act. This act establishes national standards for drinking water. The law also authorizes the EPA to regulate the injection of solid wastes into deep wells—for instance, through leakage from underground storage tanks.

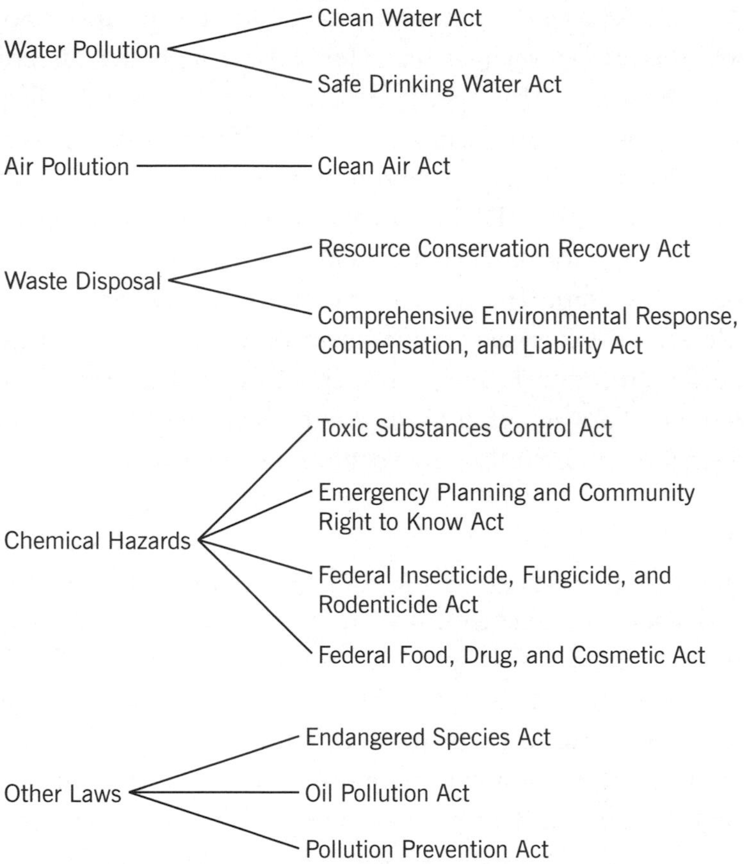

Water Pollution
— Clean Water Act
— Safe Drinking Water Act

Air Pollution ——————— Clean Air Act

Waste Disposal
— Resource Conservation Recovery Act
— Comprehensive Environmental Response, Compensation, and Liability Act

Chemical Hazards
— Toxic Substances Control Act
— Emergency Planning and Community Right to Know Act
— Federal Insecticide, Fungicide, and Rodenticide Act
— Federal Food, Drug, and Cosmetic Act

Other Laws
— Endangered Species Act
— Oil Pollution Act
— Pollution Prevention Act

Figure 4.1. The Clean Dozen.

Air Pollution

The Clean Air Act is the key legislation directed toward air pollution. Under this act, the EPA sets National Ambient Air Quality Standards (NAAQS) that limit ambient (that is, circulating) pollution. These standards are implemented by the states, which are required to develop state implementation plans (SIPs) that represent a collection of regulations that states use to control pollution.

In 1990 Congress added almost eight hundred pages of amendments to the Clean Air Act (which was originally fifty pages long). These amendments established a permit system modeled after the Clean Water Act. Your permit describes the type and amount of pollutants that you are releasing and the steps that you are taking to measure and reduce pollution. The 1990 amendments also include market-based approaches to pollution control, including pollution allowances that you can buy and sell.[8]

Waste Disposal
Two major federal laws are directed toward industrial dumping of hazardous wastes. First, the Resource Conservation and Recovery Act (RCRA) adopts a "cradle-to-grave" philosophy whereby the EPA has the power to govern the creation, storage, transport, treatment, and disposal of hazardous waste. If your company generates hazardous waste, you must obtain a permit (called a *manifest*) to store the waste at your site or ship it to an EPA-approved facility. If you own or operate a site, you must prove that you can pay for damage resulting from site operation. Even after the site is closed to further dumping, you must set aside funds to monitor and maintain the site safely. Under RCRA, the EPA also regulates your underground storage tanks.

The second law, the Comprehensive Environmental Response, Compensation, and Liability Act (CERCLA, also known as "Superfund") gives the EPA emergency powers to respond to environmental dangers from hazardous waste disposal. The EPA can order immediate removal of wastes that represent an imminent danger (for instance, from a train wreck or oil spill) and can carry out "planned removals" when the danger is substantial. Under CERCLA, the EPA will prod you to clean up sites that you have abandoned. If you refuse, the government will clean up the site and will then assess damages of up to triple the cleanup costs. Amendments to CERCLA (called the Superfund Amendment and Reauthorization Act or SARA) protect innocent landowners who make an "appropriate inquiry" into the prior uses of real estate that they purchase.

Chemical Hazards

The Toxic Substance Control Act controls the manufacture, processing, commercial distribution, use, and disposal of chemicals that pose unreasonable environmental risks. Under this law, the EPA tracks and screens the seventy-five thousand industrial chemicals that are produced or imported into the U.S.[9] You must notify the EPA ninety days before manufacturing or importing a new chemical. The EPA may require you to label your products in a certain way, keep records on your manufacturing or disposal processes, and document adverse reactions to people exposed to your chemicals. The EPA may ban substances that are especially hazardous.

Another law, the Emergency Planning and Community Right to Know Act, was enacted following a disaster in Bhopal, India, where over two thousand people died after chemicals escaped from a Union Carbide factory. This law is designed to help local communities protect the public from chemical hazards. For example, you must file information with state and local authorities about the chemicals that you use.[10]

Approximately thirty-five thousand chemical pesticides are used in the United States to eliminate insects, fungi, and rodents. Two major laws, the Federal Insecticide, Fungicide, and Rodenticide Act and the Federal Food, Drug, and Cosmetic Act, are designed to regulate these chemicals. The EPA has the right to determine whether individual pesticides balance effectiveness against safety and can ban the use of a pesticide that has an unreasonable effect on the environment. To enable the EPA to perform this function, you must provide the agency with a wealth of data about the pesticides that you manufacture, including the way they work and their side effects.

Other Major Environmental Laws

Endangered Species Act. The Endangered Species Act is designed to protect 190 threatened and 632 endangered plants and animals. The law prohibits any action that adversely affects the habitats where these species are found or that results in a "taking" of the species. For example, when the EPA reviews a pesticide, it will determine the adverse effects of the chemical on endangered species and their environment.[11]

Oil Pollution Act. This law strengthens the ability of the EPA to respond to, or prevent, oil spills. Among other features, the law requires oil storage vessels and facilities to submit plans explaining how they will respond to large oil spills. The law also provides for EPA regulation of storage facilities.[12]

Pollution Prevention Act. In 1990, Congress enacted the Pollution Prevention Act, which represents a turning point in U.S. environmental protection policy from a focus on the point where pollutants are discharged into the environment (so-called end-of-pipe or smokestack regulation) to the prevention of pollutants at their point of origin (source reduction). According to the EPA, "Source reduction is the preferred strategy for environmental protection because it often: is cost-effective; offers industry substantial savings in reduced risks to workers; and reduces risk to the environment and public health."[13] This law directs the EPA to develop a strategy to promote source reduction and to improve methods of data collection. The law also requires you to include information about source reduction at your industrial facilities in the reports that must be filed under the Emergency Planning and Community Right to Know Act.

Step Two: React to Environmental Regulation Through Flight or Fight

With the big picture perspective of environmental regulation in mind, the next step is to explore traditional flight-or-fight opportunities.

Flight
Flight in this case would require moving your business operations to another country rather than merely to another state, because federal environmental regulation in the United States applies in all states. At one time it might have been possible

for you to find other countries where environmental regulation was more lax than the U.S. variety. Today, however, there is remarkable similarity in the laws as they appear on the books.

For example, at one time companies opened plants in the People's Republic of China because a combination of substandard environmental regulations and lax enforcement resulted in lower operational costs. But in recent years, China has upgraded both its environmental laws and enforcement. For instance, you are subject to up to ten years in prison for committing an environmental crime. These new laws prompted a major U.S. company to close a plant in Jiangsu Province in 1999; the company noted that it could not operate the plant at a profit because of a new environmental law.[14]

In many countries environmental regulation is more stringent than in the United States. New forms of regulation focus on products rather than pollution caused by the manufacturing process. For example, several countries have "take-back" laws that require you to take back product packaging so that it can be reused or recycled outside the public waste disposal system.[15] A study of seventeen industrialized countries ranks the U.S. as thirteenth in the rate of progress in reducing pollution, well behind leaders such as Germany, the Netherlands, Sweden, Japan, and the United Kingdom.[16]

Fight
The traditional alternative to flight, fighting environmental regulation, takes place both before and after environmental laws and regulations are enacted. See Figure 4.2. Before a new environmental law is enacted, you have the opportunity to contribute to the public policy process by making your views known through your elected representatives, lobbyists, corporate grassroots campaigns, and political action committees.

Once a law has been enacted, Congress authorizes agencies like the EPA to create regulations that fill in the details about how the law works. An agency will first publish a proposed regulation

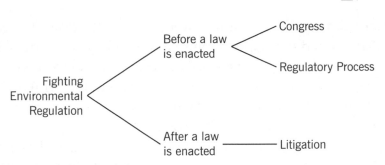

Figure 4.2. **Fighting Environmental Regulation.**

in the *Federal Register*, which will give you the opportunity to review it and provide comments. After considering your comments, and possibly revising the regulation, the EPA issues a final rule, which is then published in the Code of Federal Regulations.[17]

After a new law or regulation goes into effect, the fight often continues through the court system. A legendary case illustrates a fight before and after a final rule was adopted. Companies that produced peanut butter challenged a proposed government regulation specifying that peanut butter had to contain at least 95 percent peanut content. When this regulation was proposed in 1959, some manufacturers were producing peanut butter that contained 20–25 percent hydrogenated oils (lard). The manufacturers fought the proposed rule because a higher peanut content would increase their costs. Through a combination of tactics that included public hearings and appeals in the court system, the regulation was delayed for twelve years and, in the meantime, lowered to 90 percent peanut content.[18]

The peanut butter case was touted as a victory for manufacturers, who were able to continue manufacturing cheaper peanut butter during the twelve-year regulatory process and who eventually obtained a 5 percent reduction in the proposed peanut content. Before investing significant resources in industry activities like this, however, you should carefully analyze the costs and the benefits from a competitive advantage perspective. From a cost perspective, are your expenditures benefiting other companies that are not participating in the battle (the "free riders" described in Chapter One)? And on the benefit side, will your battle for or against a regulation give you competitive advantage vis-à-vis your competitors in the industry or will the battle, instead, improve the playing field for everyone without affecting your own competitive posture?

Even when it is clear that an environmental issue has a direct impact on your company, the cost of the fight may not be worth the benefit. For example, what would you do if someone produced a document about your company that you felt misrepresented the truth? This question faced McDonald's after London Greenpeace published a leaflet that accused McDonald's of a number of injustices, including destruction of rain forests. McDonald's identified five individuals who were responsible for the leaflet. Three of the five apologized and McDonald's decided to sue the other two, an unemployed single parent and a former gardener who had a part-time job in a pub.

Eleven years after the leaflet was published, McDonald's secured a "victory" with a judgment of approximately $98,000 against the two, although the trial judge also ruled that parts of the leaflet were true. The trial was the longest in English history and generated forty thousand documents. The two defendants were ineligible for legal aid (which is not available in libel suits in England) and defended the case without lawyers, creating a David versus Goliath scenario and considerable negative publicity for McDonald's. The trial cost McDonald's an estimated $16 million, an amount that is rising as the two defendants have taken their case to the European Court of Human Rights. In the words of one commentator: "Clearly the verdict will be enjoyed without much relish."[19] See Exhibit 4.1.

Of course, when you are defending against an agency action that has a direct impact on your company or on you as an individual, the decision regarding whether to fight is easier. For instance, a supervisor who worked for a railroad was charged

Exhibit 4.1. McLitigation Court Time and Expense.

- Trial began June 28, 1994 and ended December 13, 1996.
- 130 witnesses testified, with 40,000 pages of documents and 20,000 pages of transcripts.
- Estimated cost to McDonald's was $16 million (price of around 6.8 million Big Macs in the United States).
- Environmental activists cheered the judgment (and then left a mess of bottles, cans, and litter).

Source: Colleen Graffy, "Big Mac Bites Back," *ABA Journal*, August 1997, p. 22. Reprinted by permission of the *ABA* Journal.

with violating the Clean Water Act. The railroad had hired a contracting company to work on a project that involved using a backhoe to load rock onto railroad cars. An oil pipeline ran next to the railroad tracks where this work was performed. Parts of the pipeline had been covered before (but not after) the supervisor took over responsibility for the project. A backhoe operator accidentally hit the unprotected pipeline, causing an estimated one thousand to five thousand gallons of oil to flow into a river. The supervisor was charged with negligence in violating the Clean Water Act and was sentenced to six months in prison, six months in a halfway house, and six months of supervised release. Despite a fight that went all the way to the Supreme Court, the conviction was upheld on appeal.[20]

As these cases illustrate, there may be high stakes in a fight involving environmental matters. As a result, the search for business solutions, Step Three, becomes important.

**Step Three: Develop Business Strategies
and Solutions That Address Environmental Regulation**

As with the traditional fight described in Step Two, there are both "before" and "after" business strategies to address environmental concerns. Two strategies are useful before environmental laws and regulations are adopted, while three strategies address concerns that arise after regulations become effective. See Figure 4.3.

Before Adoption of Laws and Regulations

Two strategies that are effective before the government adopts environmental laws and regulation are negotiated rulemaking and lobbying for stronger regulation.

Use Negotiated Rulemaking. As described earlier, the traditional approach to environmental rulemaking involves notice from the EPA regarding a new rule and response from private parties in the form of comments. This process is slow and adversarial, and frequently leads to litigation. To surmount these problems, a negotiated rulemaking process (dubbed regulatory negotiation or *reg-neg*) has been developed. Under this process, regulators meet with private parties in an attempt to find shared interests and to reach consensus *before* a rule is even proposed.[21] Congress endorsed this process in 1990 with the enactment of the Negotiated Rulemaking Act.

For example, the EPA used the negotiated rulemaking process in establishing a rule relating to emission standards for ovens that process coal into coke. In January 1992, the EPA cre-

Figure 4.3. **Business Strategies for Addressing Environmental Regulations.**

ated a committee consisting of representatives of the EPA, environmental groups, the coke and steel industry, states, and unions. Meeting every two to three weeks for four months, the committee drafted a proposed rule that was published in December 1992. The final rule, which was adopted fourteen months later, has not been challenged in court.[22]

Argue for Stronger Environmental Laws. A second approach, which global companies use, is to argue for stronger environmental regulation in developing countries where they do business. For instance, the head of environmental affairs for a major corporation once told me that he had recently traveled to several less developed countries with a group of executives who held similar positions at other global firms. The purpose of the trip was to convince government officials in these countries to adopt and enforce stricter environmental laws.

This approach may seem counterintuitive, but there is a compelling logic that drives the push for higher standards. In the wake of increasing uniformity of environmental regulations worldwide, global companies often adopt global environmental standards that apply even in countries where environmental regulation is relatively weak. These high standards result in additional costs that make it difficult for global companies to compete with local firms. Strengthening local environmental law levels the playing field by forcing local companies to incur the same environmental expenses as the multinationals.[23]

After Adoption of Laws and Regulations

Three strategies are effective after environmental laws and regulations have been adopted: compliance, adoption of an environmental management system, and isolation of liability within a subsidiary.

□

Comply with Environmental Law. The compliance strategy is obvious: attempt to comply with environmental law as efficiently as possible. This strategy is sometimes described as a reactive approach, in contrast to an avoidance mentality. An article in the *Academy of Management Executive* describes the shift: "Multinational corporations (MNCs) have gone through a dramatic transformation in their approaches to environmental protection, from 1) avoiding compliance with regulatory controls during the 1960s to 2) reacting to regulatory requirements and attempting to minimize the costs of compliance."[24]

As a result of the compliance mentality "the vast majority of hard investment in cleaner and safer processes is mandated by law." The scope of this investment is significant, amounting to almost 20 percent of total capital expenditures and up to 10 percent of sales in some industries.[25] Clearly the companies that can best control this expense will have a competitive advantage.

Perhaps the most important compliance tool is an environmental audit. As the name implies, this audit is conducted to determine whether you are in compliance with environmental regulations. As a corporate attorney observed, "The audit is perhaps the best mechanism for helping management to understand and identify environmental compliance issues. It is, therefore, a management tool. . . . [An] audit will enable the company to identify, correct, and prevent the recurrence of violations, thereby avoiding liabilities."[26]

Beyond its use as a management tool, the environmental audit can result in the reduction or elimination of penalties if you promptly disclose to the EPA the results of the audit and correct violations. Since the EPA adopted its audit policy in 1996, 675 companies have disclosed violations at over 2,700 facilities and in many cases the penalties were reduced or waived. For example, GTE used the audit policy to resolve violations at 314 of its facilities in twenty-one states. Because of the company's cooperation, the penalty for these violations was $52,000 rather than $2.4 million. In 1999, seventeen other telecommunications companies discovered and corrected over 2,000 violations and were fined $178,000, a reduction of over $6 million.[27]

Many states have environmental audit privileges that shield you from being forced to disclose the audit results in an administrative or judicial proceeding. Although these privileges are laudable in encouraging the use of environmental audits, you should not allow the lack of a privilege in your state to drive your management decision about whether to conduct an audit. The audit's usefulness as a management tool will probably outweigh the risk of disclosure. Companies apparently recognize this reality, because a recent study of 988 manufacturing sites concluded that the existence of an audit privilege "does not appear to influence the level of audit activity."[28]

Even after you conduct an audit, it may be tempting to continue violating the law because of a belief that economic benefits outweigh the penalties for noncompliance. However, in setting penalties, courts and the EPA take this economic benefit into account to prevent you from gaining a competitive advantage over companies that have made investments to comply with the law. In 1999, for example, when Ashland Oil Company agreed to settle charges that several of its refineries had violated various environmental laws, $4 million of the total penalty of $5.9 million represented illegal savings.[29]

Create an Environmental Management System. An environmental management system (EMS) is defined by the EPA as "a systematic approach to ensuring that environmental activities are well managed in any organization. . . . An EMS is not fundamentally a compliance system. An EMS focuses on management systems. However, an effective EMS can be an important part of a compliance system, and can reasonably be expected to ensure and improve environmental compliance."[30]

There are many EMS models, the best known of which is ISO 14001. ISO, the International Organization for Standardization, is a Switzerland-based organization of national standards institutes, including the American National Standards Institute (ANSI). ISO finalized ISO 14001 in 1996. Companies that meet the ISO standard can "self-declare" their compliance to customers or can apply for neutral-party certification.[31] By the end of 2000, 22,897 companies had been certified in ninety-eight countries, an increase of 8,791 over the prior year.[32]

While compliance with ISO 14001 is voluntary and an EMS should be viewed primarily as a management system, there are potential external benefits, including lighter sentences if your company is convicted of an environmental offense, lower insurance premiums, and improved credit lines.[33] Compliance is also becoming a condition of doing business. For instance, in 1999 General Motors directed its suppliers to become ISO 14001-certified.[34]

While ISO 14001 is an important standard, other EMS models are also in use. In 2000, the governments of Canada, Mexico, and the United States published a list of ten elements that are compatible with many of these models, including ISO 14001.[35] These elements provide a valuable checklist when reviewing your EMS:

1. An environmental policy that is well documented and clearly communicated.
2. Communication of legal requirements and voluntary undertakings to employees and others who might affect your ability to meet these standards.
3. Environmental objectives and targets, including a timeline.
4. A structure, resources, and assignment of responsibilities to meet your objectives and targets.
5. Operational controls to meet your objectives and targets.

6. Procedures for preventing or correcting occurrences that might affect your ability to achieve your objectives and targets.
7. Appropriate training to achieve your objectives and targets.
8. Integration of the EMS into your overall planning and decision-making processes.
9. Maintenance of appropriate documentation.
10. Continuous evaluation and improvement.

Isolate Environmental Liability. The "Organizational Approach" section of Chapter Two describes the principle of limited liability as it applies to corporate shareholders. Fundamentally, a parent corporation is not liable for the debts of its subsidiaries unless the parent is directly involved in the specific activity that created the liability, or the parent does something (such as exercising such a great degree of control over the subsidiary that it is not operating independently) that leads a court to pierce the corporate veil that normally protects the parent from liability.

These principles apply in the environmental arena. For instance, the United States claimed that a parent corporation, CPC, was responsible under CERCLA for the costs of cleaning up environmental damage caused by its subsidiary, Ott Chemical, which was bankrupt. In reviewing this case (and sending it back to the trial court for further proceedings), the Supreme Court determined that CERCLA did not change general principles of corporate law. In the words of the Court, CPC would not be liable for the damage caused by Ott Chemical "unless the corporate veil may be pierced . . . [or unless CPC] actively participated in, and exercised control over, the operations of the facility itself."[36]

The clear message from this decision is that you can protect your parent corporation from environmental liability created by your subsidiaries if you take a hands-off approach and allow them to operate independently.

Step Four: Climb to the Balcony—Reframe
Environmental Regulations as a Business Opportunity

Step Three (the search for business strategies to address environmental regulation) is necessary for all companies but not sufficient to gain competitive advantage. The fundamental limitation of Step Three is that these strategies relate to compliance with environmental regulations and these regulations, in turn, concentrate on end-of-pipe controls. Focusing on these regulations may cause you to overlook significant opportunities to move ahead of your competitors. When you climb the balcony for a broader perspective, you should ask this fundamental business question: Forgetting about legal requirements, does a green strategy create opportunities to lower costs and to increase revenue?

As noted in an article in the *Academy of Management Executive,* multinational corporations have decided that the answer to this question is yes, as they have progressed from avoiding compliance to reacting to environmental regulations in an attempt to minimize compliance costs to trying to turn environmental problems into opportunities.[37] For instance, 3M notes, "Achieving 100 percent compliance is a critical issue to 3M because we are required to deal with thousands of governmental regulations worldwide every day." But the company also attempts to go "beyond legal requirements, in part by developing environmental management plans that merge environmental goals with business strategy."[38]

There are four linked approaches to consider as you attempt to move from a reactive to a proactive posture. In considering these approaches, the economic context of your decisions and actions is especially important. As Harvard professor Forest Reinhardt has wisely observed, instead of asking whether it pays to be green, you should ask what circumstances might make it pay: "A business's behavior with respect to the environment, like any other aspect of strategy or management, should be considered in the light of the basic economic situation of the business: the structure of the industry in which it competes, its own position within that industry, and its internal organizational capabilities."[39]

Make a Commitment to Sustainable Development
The first of the four approaches is perhaps the most important. Your company should move from a compliance mentality to a strategy of commitment to a sustainable development. *Sustainable development* is defined by the World Commission on Environment and Development as "that which meets the needs of the present without compromising the ability of future generations to meet their own needs."[40] By planting a stake in the ground through your commitment to this strategy and making it a high priority, you may be able to change the mindset of your employees in ways that will encourage them to think creatively about new products and processes while at the same time developing company pride.

One statement of commitment to sustainable development is this description of DuPont by CEO Charles Holliday: "DuPont is a science company that is focused on *sustainable growth*—creating shareholder and societal value while decreasing our environmental footprint" (his emphasis).[41] In recognition of the fact that investors diversify their holdings to include companies committed to sustainable development, Dow Jones created a Sustainability Group Index in 1999. The Index consists of over two hundred companies (including DuPont) with a total market capitalization of over $5 trillion, representing the top 10 percent in sustainability in sixty-four industry groups. In recent years, these companies have significantly outperformed the Dow Jones World Index of companies.[42] The Web sites of these companies are a gold mine of information about best practices in sustainable development.

Some companies have gone beyond a commitment to a sustainable environment and have made stewardship of the environment a core business purpose. Often these are smaller firms like Patagonia, which has a goal of restoring nature while pro-viding high-performance gear.[43] Patagonia pledges 1 percent of sales or 10 percent of pretax profits, whichever is higher, to grassroots environmental groups.[44] But some larger companies also come close to making environmental stewardship a core purpose. The CEO of DuPont, for instance, talks in terms of "sustainable growth for stakeholders" and the company has promised that, by 2010, one-quarter of its revenue will come from non-depletable resources.[45]

Select a Framework for Strategy Implementation

Once you have made a commitment to a sustainable environ-ment, you should select a framework for considering the specific options that will be reviewed in the next section. Your selection of a framework, and specific options that flow from it, should never stray far from what Porter calls the "two basic types of competitive advantage a firm can possess: low cost or differen-tiation."[46] In other words, will your environmental framework enable you to be a cost leader in your industry or to produce products and services that are unique? Your framework might be based on one of the following three state-of-the-art models, or you might develop your own framework to meet your par-ticular cost and differentiation goals.

World Business Council for Sustainable Development (WBCSD). In 1991, WBC coined a word to describe sustainable development from a business perspective: *eco-efficiency.* The WBCSD defines this word as "creating more goods and services with ever less use of resources, waste and pollution."[47] The objective of eco-efficiency is to increase the value of your products and services while at the same time reducing your business's consumption of resources and impact on nature. The WBCSD implementation framework addresses four areas:[48]

- Reengineer your processes to reduce resource consumption and pollution while saving costs.
- Cooperate with other companies to add value to your by-products.
- Redesign your products.
- Rethink your markets to find new ways to meet customer needs.

World Resources Institute (WRI). According to the WRI business value model, there are several reasons why companies adopt sustainable development strategies. These reasons include reducing costs and liabilities, and increasing customer loyalty and market position (by adding environmental benefits to products while at the same time outperforming competitors in meeting customer needs).[49]

The WRI framework includes three ideas:

- Do more with fewer resources—for example, by using knowledge and technology to reduce your use of materials.
- Improve your bottom line from nature—for instance, by using natural processes to reduce waste, as discussed later in this chapter under process redesign.
- Build connections with the community in which you operate, which may enable you to develop trust and identify emerging markets.[50]

Natural Capitalism. Amory Lovins and L. Hunter Lovins of the Rocky Mountain Institute and Paul Hawken, the founder of the retailer Smith and Hawken, have developed an approach they call "natural capitalism" for improving the environment, profits, and competitiveness. Writing in the *Harvard Business Review* (in an article that should be required reading for any manager seriously concerned about the environment),[51] they discuss the four interrelated changes in business practice that express the intent of natural capitalism:

- Increase the productivity of natural resources through design and technology.
- Shift to production models that are based on nature's designs, so that output is either "returned harmlessly to the ecosystem as a nutrient, like compost, or becomes an input for manufacturing another product."[52]
- Move to a business model that is based on a flow of services rather than the sale of goods.
- Recognize that the ecosystem underlies your business success by reinvesting in natural capital.

Select Specific Actions for Meeting Your Commitment
to a Sustainable Development Strategy
Once you have selected or developed a framework for thinking about specific options, it is time to consider possible actions that will enable you to pursue your sustainable development goals. The experiences of other companies, such as those described here, provide a menu of best practices. These practices are organized using common themes drawn from the three frameworks just described. Fundamentally, the frameworks have an overarching "R and R" focus on redesign and reinvestment in the environment. See Figure 4.4.

Redesign Your Processes. Three types of process redesign have received considerable attention. The first type focuses on minimizing and preventing waste (as opposed to coping with it via end-of-pipeline controls). Over a four-year period, for instance, General Dynamics eliminated close to forty million pounds of hazardous waste discharge, and in three years Chevron reduced its hazardous waste by 60 percent, which saved the company

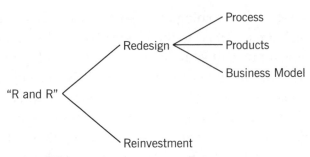

Figure 4.4. **Menu of Best Practices.**

over $10 million in disposal costs.[53] According to a recent study, beyond direct savings, manufacturing performance improved in plants that increased their investment in pollution prevention; performance declined in plants that stressed pollution control instead.[54] Results from another study suggest that the companies most successful in reducing toxic chemical emissions (as measured by an EPA database) outperform other companies in returns on sales and assets.[55]

The second type of process redesign emphasizes lean manufacturing. Lean manufacturing is based on four elements of "lean thinking" described in the book with that title by James Womack and Daniel Jones: "the *continuous flow* of value, as *defined* by the customer, at the *pull* of the customer, in search of *perfection*."[56] (The emphasis is in the original quotation.) Sometimes old-fashioned common sense will enable you to achieve leaner manufacturing, once your sustainable environment goal is in place. Advocates of natural capitalism cite the example of Interface Corporation, the world's largest commercial carpet company. Through two simple design changes in the system used to manufacture carpets at a factory in Shanghai, the company reduced its power requirements by 92 percent.[57]

The third type of process redesign emphasizes our role within the natural world. This form of process redesign requires an understanding of the distinction between "biological nutrients," which are returned to biological systems, and "technical nutrients," which are returned to the production cycle. An example of a biological nutrient is upholstery fabric developed for Design Tex that, when removed from an old chair, decomposes naturally on a compost pile. Technical nutrients are illustrated by Interface Corporation's design of a carpet that can be completely recycled (as opposed to more typical recycling that reduces the quality of material as it is reused). A customer who wants to replace the carpet will return it (the "technical nutrient") and the company will then provide a new one in the customer's choice of color.[58]

Redesign Your Products. Product redesign encompasses three principles. The first principle is that product design is increasingly important to gaining competitive advantage. For example, after DuPont's agricultural division developed a new type of biodegradable herbicide that allowed a dramatic reduction in herbicides per acre, DuPont rose from seventh to second in the industry.[59]

Product design for competitive advantage gained impetus after a 1998 Executive Order in which President Clinton directed all federal agencies to use EPA guidelines for environmentally preferable purchasing. "Environmentally preferable" was defined by the president to mean "products or services that have a lesser or reduced effect on human health and the environment when compared with competing products or services."[60] This order is especially significant because the U.S. government is the largest consumer of goods and services in the country, and probably the world, with expenditures of over $200 billion annually.[61] Companies that redesign their products to be environmentally preferable will achieve greater success in dealing with this gigantic customer.

The second principle of product redesign is to consider a product's entire life cycle. The life cycle includes everything from the acquisition of raw materials through the customer's use and disposal of the product.[62] As noted earlier, this concept is already embedded in the law of several countries that require companies to take back product packaging so that it can be recycled without impact on the public waste disposal system. Many companies are not waiting for these laws to be enacted in their own countries before adopting take-back policies. For instance, Sonoco, one of the world's largest manufacturers of packaging materials, recycles almost two million tons of paper annually, and many of its products are made entirely from recycled material. By recycling almost 62,000 wooden reels in a recent year, the company saved over 20,500 trees and almost 76,000 cubic yards of landfill space.[63] Figure 4.5 illustrates 3M's life cycle management process.

The third principle is value creation. A focus on life cycle will not be sufficient to create competitive advantage unless your environmentally redesigned products create value for your customers. For example, horizontal axis washing machines are environmentally friendly in that they need less detergent and less

Life Cycle Stage / Impact	Material Acquisition	R&D Operations	Manufacturing Operations	Customer Needs	
				Use	Disposal
Environment					
Energy/ Resources					
Health					
Safety					

Figure 4.5. Life Cycle Management Process.
Source: "3M Worldwide." Available online: http://www.3m.com/about3m/environment/policies_prod_respon.jhtml. Used by permission.

water than vertical axis machines. But they are also popular with customers because they clean clothes better, are smaller, and can be raised off the floor. An insecticide developed by SC Johnson brings benefits to the environment (uses half the volatile organic compound of competing products) and to the customer (smells better, won't ignite, and leaves less residue).[64]

Value creation for your customers often translates into value creation for your shareholders. For instance, the SC Johnson insecticide saves the company $2 million each year in manufacturing costs. And semiconductor firms have shown that reducing product size can increase profits. As noted by the CEO of DuPont: "Those firms make ever smaller products, but because they deliver more benefits they make bigger profits overall." A case in point is a DuPont product, polyester films. New films are half as thick as before but, because they are stronger, they sell at a price that is almost six times greater than the thicker film.[65]

Redesign Your Business Model. Redesigning your business model creates exciting and far-reaching opportunities for seizing competitive advantage. Your redesign process should focus on two basic questions. First, what business are you in? Second, are new forms of alliances possible with your suppliers and customers?

Answering the first question requires a hard look at customer needs. If you manufacture carpets, for example, you might understandably consider yourself in the business of selling carpets. But your customers do not necessarily want to buy carpets. Instead, they may simply want a floor surface that is functional, warm, attractive, and comfortable. If you focus on these needs, fundamental changes in your business model may come to mind that can significantly improve the environment.

For instance, Interface Corporation, the carpet manufacturing company mentioned previously, has developed a new business model called the Evergreen Service Agreement in which its customers lease rather than purchase carpeting. This program is designed to meet customer needs while enabling them to avoid large capital expenditures. The program covers the complete life cycle of the product, from initial installation through periodic rejuvenation to reclamation for recycling. Replacing only the worn parts of carpeting reduces material consumption by an estimated 80 percent and energy savings "from not producing a whole new carpet is in itself enough to produce all the carpeting that the new business model requires."[66] The company's CEO also serves as the "chief environmental officer." In the company's words: "Sustainability is part of our strategic approach to competitive advantage."[67]

Beyond leasing, there may be other opportunities to change your business model from a product to a service orientation. In some cases, you might be able to add an environmentally related service to your product line. For example, Kodak Environmental Services helps customers with regulatory compliance and recycling. Beyond benefits to the environment, services like these generate customer loyalty and make it difficult for your customers to switch to your competitors.[68]

Your search for a new business model might lead to a more fundamental change if you decide to sell a service instead of a product. For instance, suppose that you are in the business of selling paint to automotive companies. In analyzing your customers' real needs, you determine that, strictly speaking, they aren't interested in buying paint but that they do need painted cars. The solution? You operate their paint shop, getting paid for each car painted rather than for each gallon of paint sold. The environmental benefit? With this new model, your incentives shift to a search for ways to reduce expended paint. Within two years after DuPont took over operation of a Ford Paint shop in the United Kingdom, the company was able to save around 8 percent in material costs, and its U.K. market share in this business jumped from 25 percent to 75 percent.[69]

The second question that you should ask in redesigning your business model is whether new forms of alliances are possible with your suppliers and customers. A fundamental business goal of such alliances is to make the value chain as efficient as possible by eliminating unnecessary transactions. This goal serves environmental purposes as well by reducing resource needs.[70] Alliances also allow for other environmental benefits. Because one company's waste can be another company's raw material or power source, new industrial parks match companies that can use one another's waste. Some companies have even developed markets for waste. Anheuser-Busch, for instance, sells waste from its breweries as fertilizer.[71]

Alliances are not limited to the value chain. Dow Chemical, for instance, has entered into an unusual collaboration with environmental activists. Working with the National Resources Defense Council, Dow asked five of its critics to review the company's business needs and processes in an attempt to find ways to cut waste. As a result, "Dow is on track to cut production of a list of toxic chemicals selected by the environmentalists by 37 percent and to reduce the release of the chemicals into the air or water by 43 percent."[72]

Reinvestment in the Environment. Reinvestment in the environment is based on the fundamental business principle that you must reinvest earnings in your capital and the recognition that the natural environment represents an important form of business capital. Companies that invest in nature's capital are gaining new forms of competitive advantage. For example, companies in the wood products industry have learned that certification by the Forest Stewardship Council can lead to extra profits, while customer concerns about clear-cutting practices can lead to a significant loss of business.[73]

A new form of entrepreneur, dubbed the "enviro-capitalist," is taking reinvestment one step further by using business techniques to preserve the environment. For instance, a paper company must wait thirty years for its investment in a forest to mature. In the past, during this time period a company received no profits and incurred various costs, including litter, off-road traffic, and other by-products of increasing public use of forests. Enter Tom Bourland, a wildlife manager and entrepreneur for International Paper. Bourland developed a fee-based recreation program that meets the needs of people who are interested in a wilderness experience while also producing a profit for the company.[74]

Implement the Actions You Select
After selecting possible actions, it is time to focus on implementation. Under the philosophy that "what gets measured gets done," accounting and reporting are especially important activities in measuring your implementation progress and establishing credibility. Full cost accounting (FCA), also known as environmental accounting, is an important management tool because it identifies all the costs associated with a product or process. With FCA, the costs assigned to a painting process might include not only direct costs, like paint and equipment, but also indirect costs such as waste disposal, regulatory paperwork, insurance costs and other items that are usually considered "overhead."[75] For example, several employees of a control valve manufacturer, concerned about hazardous waste produced by conventional coatings, proposed alternative coatings using traditional accounting. Their proposal was rejected because it did not improve profitability. They then did a full cost accounting that included waste costs. With this approach, management was able to see the positive impact and supported the proposal.[76]

Among other decision-making tools for internal management use are the eco-efficiency indicators developed by the WBCSD. Eco-efficiency ratios are calculated through the use of an equation that divides the value of a product or service by its influence on the environment. The WBCSD has developed a

Performance Platform that includes the eco-efficiency ratios for a number of companies.[77]

The Coalition for Environmentally Responsible Economies (CERES) has also been active in establishing reporting guidelines. Over fifty companies have endorsed the CERES principles, ranging from large firms like General Motors and Coca Cola to smaller companies like Timberland and Aveda Corporation. By endorsing these principles, companies agree to complete annual CERES reports that are available to the public.[78]

CHAPTER SUMMARY

The government represents a key stakeholder in your business success. As this chapter on environmental protection illustrates, the Manager's Legal Plan creates opportunities for competitive advantage even when you are confronted with ubiquitous and expensive governmental regulation.

Step One. Gain a basic understanding of the legal structure of environmental regulation. This chapter provides an overview of the key clusters of environmental law: water pollution, air pollution, waste disposal, and chemical hazards.

Step Two. Explore traditional flight and fight response mechanisms. Flight is no longer a realistic response because federal law is pervasive within the United States, and laws elsewhere increasingly mimic or exceed U.S. requirements. Fighting environmental regulation takes place before laws or regulations are enacted or afterward, through litigation. In considering a fight at either stage, you must determine whether your firm is bearing more than its share of costs (thus benefiting free riders in your industry) and whether winning a regulatory battle on behalf of your industry will provide any real competitive advantage for your firm.

Step Three. Consider business strategies and solutions that address environmental regulation from "before" and "after" perspectives. Two approaches used by companies before a new law or regulation is adopted are negotiated rulemaking and intensive lobbying for stricter environmental regulations in countries where enforcement has historically been lax. After adoption of environmental laws and regulations, compliance becomes the dominant strategy. The environmental audit, a key compliance tool, can reduce or even eliminate legal penalties. Beyond an audit, an environmental management system can produce business and legal benefits. And through the use of parent-subsidiary structures, you can isolate environmental risks and protect the parent corporation from devastating loss.

Step Four. Reframe environmental regulation as a business opportunity and use four key approaches that are critical to achieving competitive advantage:

1. Move from a compliance mentality to a sustainable development strategy.
2. Develop a framework for selecting the specific actions that will enable you to achieve your strategic goals. This chapter includes three leading frameworks based on eco-efficiency, business value, and natural capitalism models.
3. Select from among four types of actions: redesign of processes, products, and business models, and reinvestment in the environment. *Process redesign* includes pollution prevention, lean manufacturing, and the use of biological or technical nutrients. *Product redesign* focuses on the entire life cycle of your products and the value they bring to customers. *Business model redesign* emphasizes an understanding of your customers' underlying needs and possibilities for alliances. *Reinvestment in the environment* includes new forms of entrepreneurship developed by so-called enviro-capitalists.
4. Implement your chosen actions, using management tools such as full cost accounting and eco-efficiency indicators.

Chapters Two, Three, and Four have applied the Manager's Legal Plan to specific topics that head the list of a manager's legal concerns: product liability, workers' compensation, wrongful discharge, sexual harassment, and environmental regulation. The book concludes in Chapter Five with an examination of three broader concerns that create opportunities for competitive advantage across the spectrum of legal issues that you face. These concerns are legal resources, management tools, and the creation of an ethical corporate culture.

Questions to Consider

1. Do you use an environmental audit to determine whether you are in compliance with environmental regulations?
2. Do you have an environmental management system in place that includes the ten elements in the checklist presented earlier in this chapter?
3. Has your company developed a framework, perhaps using one of the models suggested in this chapter, for implementing its environmental strategy?
4. Have you selected specific actions from the menu provided in this chapter that will enable you to achieve your environmental goals?
5. Do you use accounting and reporting tools to measure the success of your actions?

Resources, Tools, and Values

E arlier chapters of this book describe the Manager's Legal Plan and illustrate how the plan creates competitive advantage when used to address several of the most vexing problems in business: product liability, workers' compensation, wrongful discharge, and sexual harassment, and environmental regulation.

This concluding chapter will address general concerns that create opportunities for competitive advantage across a broad range of legal matters. The chapter encompasses three topics: legal resources that you need to seize competitive advantage, managers' tools that are useful when you work with corporate attorneys on business/legal problems, and the creation of an ethical corporate culture. In each of these areas, companies have developed conventional business strategies to address legal problems. But the focus on specific strategies has caused many companies to overlook big picture issues that become apparent with a trip to the balcony.

■ Legal Resources

This section first reviews conventional strategies for developing and using legal resources. Then it turns to new opportunities for using these resources for competitive advantage.

Conventional Business Strategies for Developing and Using Legal Resources

In a world where law touches every aspect of business operations and decision making, you need high-quality legal resources to seize competitive advantage. According to an article in the *Harvard Business Review:* "A decade of growth in the scope, nature, and complexity of government regulation has catapulted attorneys into daily business operations to an unprecedented degree. The equally rapid rise in consumer, shareholder, employee, and competitor litigation has forced prudent managers to include legal advice as an essential element of business planning and decision making."[1] Recognizing the importance of sound legal advice, companies face two fundamental questions relating to their legal resources (see Figure 5.1). First, should the company develop an in-house legal staff or rely on outside law firms? Second, how can the company control legal costs?

Make or Buy Legal Services?
The first question is essentially a make or buy decision: Should you create your own legal resources inside the company or buy outside legal resources? As a general rule, companies outsource

Figure 5.1. Legal Resources: Basic Concerns.

business activities that do not provide "competitive superiority." They should not outsource activities that "create and capture value," "neutralize environmental threats," or "stimulate the development of new capabilities and competencies."[2] As discussed in earlier chapters, the legal environment in which business operates contains a number of threats, such as product liability and workers' compensation, that can be neutralized through sound legal advice. And a later part of this chapter will discuss the key role that in-house lawyers play in creating value and developing new capabilities.

Consequently, while your company will inevitably continue to buy some legal services, an in-house law department is essential to achieving competitive advantage. Even a small company will benefit from having an in-house attorney, who may perform multiple roles (for example, combining the roles of corporate attorney and chief financial officer or corporate attorney and human resource director).

The value of an in-house law department is demonstrated by surveys of senior executive satisfaction with legal services. For instance, a survey of CEOs and other senior executives, reported in *Corporate Counsel* in 2001, concluded that 67 percent ranked their law department's performance as "excellent," while only 15 percent gave this rating to their outside lawyers. Among the top reasons why these executives have an in-house law department: in-house lawyers understand the company better than outside lawyers and they participate in strategic planning.[3] It is no accident that General Electric, a company that perennially heads the rankings of the world's most admired and most respected companies,[4] also has the world's leading law department.[5]

What credentials should you look for in hiring in-house lawyers? Graduation from a reputable law school and experience in dealing with business law issues are important attributes. Membership and active involvement in an association of in-house lawyers also signals the potential for success as an in-house attorney. The premier association of in-house lawyers is the American Corporate Counsel Association (ACCA). Founded in 1982, ACCA has been a leader in developing approaches that, from a legal perspective, enable companies to achieve competitive advantage. Membership in ACCA provides in-house attorneys with a treasure trove of benchmarking materials, as well as sample forms, guidelines, policies, and the *ACCA DOCKET*, the leading journal devoted to increasing the value that in-house counsel add to their companies.

What Mechanisms Are Available to Control Legal Costs?
As discussed in Chapter One, cost control is essential to achieving competitive advantage. In-house attorneys, of course, have primary responsibility for controlling in-house legal costs. An especially important example is the use of alternative dispute resolution, which is covered later in this chapter.

In-house attorneys also play an important role in evaluating the quality and cost of the outside legal services that are necessary even when your company has established a strong in-house department. Among the alternatives to traditional hourly billing that have been developed in recent years are the following:[6]

1. *Flat Rate.* You agree to pay the law firm a fixed amount for a transaction or other legal service, such as $100,000 for a trial.

A variation of the flat rate is project billing, whereby a flat fee is charged for a specific assignment, such as drafting a contract. Another variation is incentive billing, whereby the law firm receives a bonus beyond the flat rate for specified results.

2. *Fee Cap.* The law firm charges you an hourly rate but the total bill will be capped at an agreed-upon amount.

3. *Blended Rate.* Law firm partners normally receive an hourly rate that is higher than junior lawyers. With a blended rate, you pay a single hourly rate somewhere between the partner and junior lawyer rates, regardless of who does the work.

4. *Defense Contingency Fee.* Contingency fees, traditionally used in hiring plaintiffs' attorneys, can also be used by companies when they hire defense attorneys. The law firm's compensation depends on the case results. For example, the firm might receive a percentage of the amount saved in litigation.

5. *Requests for Proposals.* You invite several law firms to bid on a particular project. For instance, New York Life Insurance Co. asks firms competing for its business to submit a bid after providing the firms with an RFP that includes an analysis of past legal expenses.[7]

6. *Legal Audits.* You can hire an outside organization to audit the billings from your law firm. According to an article in *Risk Management,* the best of "the legal cost control methods available to risk managers . . . remains a law firm audit from a carefully chosen vendor."[8]

However, the use of these alternatives can create tension between in-house and outside lawyers. The alternatives have also produced mixed results, as illustrated by Wal-Mart's experience. Wal-Mart's aggressive use of flat fees and other alternatives has been called the "Wal-Mart-ization of the law." As noted by the company's general counsel, "The plan isn't to give you [outside attorneys] so much money that you can send your kid to college in a Porsche. . . . A good old Chevrolet will do."[9]

On one hand, it appears that the alternatives have not affected the company's success in court: "Plaintiffs who sue Wal-Mart usually walk away empty-handed."[10] On the other hand, Wal-Mart has been sanctioned in a number of cases for "discovery abuse"—that is, failure to produce evidence. Why? Plaintiffs' attorneys claim that flat fee arrangements may cause outside lawyers to skimp "on case preparation and [avoid] digging for evidence by claiming that the evidence doesn't exist."[11]

New Perspectives on Legal Resources

The two questions just discussed (in-house versus outsourced legal resources and controlling costs) apply to every business function, not just law. But the attention devoted to these questions, especially the cost control issue as applied to legal resources, might cause you to overlook broader issues that create powerful opportunities to use legal resources to achieve competitive advantage. These broader issues cluster around the three questions reflected in Figure 5.2: Are your company attorneys focused on your customers? Are your in-house attorneys using best practices adapted from other areas of your business? Can the law department be developed into a profit center? After addressing these questions, this section will close with a checklist for evaluating the quality of your law department.

Figure 5.2. Legal Resources: New Concerns.

The Customers of Your Company Attorneys

Customer focus is important for any business function. In the corporate legal community, for instance, there has been considerable debate over the following question, raised by a participant in a panel discussion of corporate lawyers: "I report to the president, who reports to the CEO of our Parisian parent. We have a board of four directors. But who is my client? Is my client the president? Is my client 'the company'? Is my client the executive staff?"

Corporate counsel often disagree on the answer to this question. For instance, one panelist responded, "My client is the president." Another answered, "The shareholders." Still another panelist stated, "My client is the corporation."[12] According to the American Bar Association's Model Rules of Professional Conduct, the correct—although still fuzzy—answer is that a lawyer hired by an organization (say, your company) represents the organization.

This issue has practical implications that relate to attorney-client privilege, the rule that protects communications between attorney and client from involuntary disclosure when these communications relate to legal advice. The privilege is fraught with perils. For instance, a survey of corporate officers and directors at *Fortune* 100 companies revealed that over 40 percent did not know "that the communications had to be confidential." Even more surprising—and directly related to the question of determining who is the corporate attorney's client—is the finding that most executives "erroneously believe that corporate counsel personally represents them when they speak with corporate counsel on matters relating to their corporate responsibilities." This belief could lead "to personal liability. . . . [and] to employees being offered up in sacrifice to the greater corporate good."[13]

Understanding whom the attorney represents is important to both corporate attorneys and managers, but the problem is that another stakeholder—the customer—has been completely ignored. Because competitive advantage requires that companies create value for their customers, the "big C" *Clients* of your attorneys are your customers, even though the attorneys' client in a narrower legal sense is the corporation. In a market-oriented company, your attorneys—like everyone—must focus on the customer.

Some companies take this idea very seriously. For example, picture yourself as a young attorney who has just graduated from a prestigious law school near the top of your class. You are hired by the law department at McDonald's Corporation and look forward to becoming an expert on the legal intricacies of franchise law and site acquisition. Your first assignment? Put on your apron and flip hamburgers for two weeks in a McDonald's restaurant. Your next assignment? Attend McDonald's training program, Hamburger University, where you will supplement your Juris Doctor degree with a Bachelor of Hamburgerology degree. As Shelby Yastrow, general counsel for McDonald's, notes, "Every lawyer on our litigation team spends hours in our restaurants, because we sometimes have to explain why a licensee is not being renewed or not getting another restaurant. We have to understand how the business is run, so we get in there and cook hamburgers."[14]

Once you begin your work as a McDonald's lawyer, your education about the business continues, as you will be asked to serve on projects that have little or nothing to do with the law. Again according to Shelby Yastrow, this experience will "give you a better understanding of the company, but much more importantly will demonstrate that you are a business person who happens to bring something extra to the table, namely legal talent, not a technocrat who is more interested in the nicety of the law than in corporate profits."[15] The McDonald's legal philosophy is symbolized by the fact that the company motto of "Quality, service, and cleanliness" is reflected on lawyers' notepads, which state: "Less Esq., more QSC. More burgers, less BS."[16]

Similar approaches used by other companies include placing legal staff on-site (known as co-location) to encourage them to develop business judgment, and bringing outside counsel into the company for one-year internships so that they better understand the business.[17]

Certain risks arise when the distinction between legal advice and business advice becomes blurred. For example, the business advice provided by attorneys is not protected by attorney-client privilege, a major concern at many companies. But McDonald's, while doing everything possible to maintain the privilege, opts to retain intense focus on the customer. Again quoting McDonald's attorney Shelby Yastrow: "I am there for the same reason everybody else is: to sell hamburgers, open restaurants, and get a return for our shareholders."[18]

Using Best Practices from Other Areas of Your Business
The traditional philosophy regarding the law department was that, because of the complexity and uncertainty inherent in the law, you couldn't manage lawyers using conventional approaches. As a CEO once joked, the law department is the only one with an unlimited budget—and each year the department exceeds its budget.[19] While the law department does face unique challenges, your big-picture perspective from the balcony should enable you to identify opportunities to improve the management of the department in ways that makes your company more competitive.

Consider, for example, the challenge faced by the DuPont law department. In 1991, the department handled close to twelve hundred cases and the caseload was increasing at a rate of 20 percent to 40 percent annually. To handle this volume of cases, DuPont attorneys worked with around 350 law firms across the

United States. As DuPont attorneys struggled to handle this huge caseload without dramatically increasing legal costs, they received a mandate from the DuPont CEO. He advised them that the company must cut expenses by $1 billion and the law department had to share in the cost cutting.[20]

The first reaction of DuPont's in-house attorneys to this mandate was fairly conventional. After benchmarking other law departments, they called the company's outside law firms and told them to reduce their fees.

But DuPont attorneys soon realized that reducing fees would not accomplish their cost-cutting goals, so they turned to a more radical approach. When they examined business practices within the company, they discovered that the procurement staff was able to obtain volume discounts and improve quality by reducing the number of suppliers. Using this basic concept, the attorneys developed a strategy called the DuPont Legal Model, which is built on strategic partnering with its outside law firms. According to DuPont attorney Daniel Mahoney, "The hallmark of these relationships [with outside firms] is a shift from simple cost-cutting, which will negatively affect law firm profits and ultimately attorney-client relationships, to one of value enhancement where the client and the law firm share in the benefits of efficient, results-oriented legal services."[21]

Here are the key elements of the DuPont implementation plan:

1. Reduction of the number of law firms from around 350 to 34 so-called Primary Law Firms (PLFs).[22]
2. Use of technology to improve communication and share knowledge among the PLFs.
3. Process redesign to develop systematic approaches to case management.
4. Performance metrics to measure success in reducing costs and improving quality.

5. Training that leverages the knowledge of in-house and out-
    side attorneys.[23]

Not everyone initially appreciated the benefits of the plan.
As one attorney noted during a training session, "If we were interested in numbers we would be accountants."[24] But the results
are impressive. According to DuPont attorney Thomas Sager, the
company reduced legal expenses by an estimated $72.5 million
from 1994 to 1997. The law department was also able to cut its
caseload in half, while reducing cycle time from thirty-nine to
twenty-two months.[25]

The plan has produced a win-win result in that PLFs also
benefit from improved cash flow, reduction in marketing costs,
positive publicity, networking opportunities, and technology
and information advantages.[26] According to James Leader, a
partner in one of the PLFs, "We win, too, not only because of the
guaranteed business, but because DuPont has helped us to improve technology, referred other clients, and encouraged us to
cooperate with other law firms in ways we never would have
imagined a few years ago."[27]

The DuPont Legal Model illustrates the potential benefits to
your company when the law department uses best practices developed in other areas of the company. Technology, especially,
has the potential to transform traditional lawyer-client relationships. For example, companies have come to realize that the legal
education of their employees is important to achieving competitive advantage. As a result, companies like Lucent Technologies
have created online courses on business law for employees. According to Lucent attorney Philip Crowley, employees who understand legal issues "are more likely to recognize business
situations that call for a lawyer's expertise."[28]

Computer-based collaboration is also important to corporate attorneys, especially given the impact of globalization of the
law discussed in Chapter One. Cisco Systems, for instance, has

created Legal Exchange, which enables, say, an attorney in Asia, to obtain immediate advice from Cisco attorneys around the world. Other uses of technology include online contract management, legal self-diagnostic programs that enable employees to obtain legal advice after answering a series of questions, and on-line auctions to select outside law firms.[29]

The Law Department as a Profit Center

Earlier chapters have explored the role that law can play in enabling your company to gain competitive advantage. For example, a product liability analysis of how your customers actually use your products may identify needs that are not being met. And environmental regulation may create new customer needs that lead to new product opportunities. In the words of Ben Heineman, General Electric general counsel, a key goal of the law department's Six Sigma program is to "creatively enhance revenue and profit for the business unit we're working with."[30]

If law departments can contribute to the success of profit centers, why not also consider possibilities for them to become profit centers in their own right? According to Julie Davis, who manages Andersen's Intellectual Asset Consulting Practice, "It's not enough that [law departments] keep their company out of legal trouble; they must now think of ways to contribute to the bottom line and increase shareholder value."[31] When *Corporate Counsel* magazine convened an advisory group (called LD21) of leading corporate counsel to examine the role of the law department in the twenty-first century, one of their conclusions was that: "Many law departments can become profit centers by using their resources to build new customer relationships."[32]

Let's say, for example, that you work for a typical manufacturing company. When you step back, climb to the balcony, and view your company assets from a big picture perspective, what do you see? If someone asked you this question in the 1980s, your response would have been "factories and equipment," which at that time represented most of a manufacturing firm's market value. Those assets currently account for less than a third of market value. Today, even at manufacturing firms, the most valuable asset is intellectual property.[33] Your company's development, protection, and use of this key asset are critical to competitive advantage.

In 1990, the fifty patent attorneys employed by Xerox "operated defensively. There was no special unit that ripped apart competitor's products to root out patent infringement, for example. Nor were legal staff assigned to pursue infringers."[34] That approach is still dominant at most companies today.[35]

However, some companies are adopting a more aggressive posture toward intellectual property, and their law departments should play leadership roles in transforming this attitude into action. There are two key aspects to the new intellectual property strategy. First, companies must attack competitors who infringe upon their intellectual property rights. Second, they must identify and market intellectual property that would otherwise waste away on the company shelf.

The first aspect of the new strategy requires a recognition that the business benefits of pursuing infringers often far outweigh what might appear to be the substantial legal cost of litigation. It is not surprising that "plaintiff" has been called the fifth "P" of marketing (joining product, price, promotion, and placement),[36] as the number of new intellectual property cases tripled between 1996 and 1999.[37] Xerox, for example, has become so aggressive in pursuing infringers that a competitor has charged the company with moving "marketplace competition into the courtroom."[38]

The success of the aggressive strategy is illustrated by TYLENOL's courtroom battles. McNeil Laboratories has actively filed suit to prevent companies from interfering with its trademark. For example, McNeil obtained a preliminary injunction that prevented American Home Products from launching

EXTRANOL, a product that would have competed with its own new product, EXTRA-STRENGTH TYLENOL. McNeil obtained an injunction that prevented Kroger from selling non-aspirin pain relievers named ACTENOL, SUPERNOL, and HYDENOL. And through settlement of litigation, the company forced a competitor to drop "nol" from a product initially called FEVERNOL.[39]

The second aspect of the new intellectual property strategy—identifying and marketing intellectual property—illustrates more directly the role that the law department can play in generating profits. It is estimated that companies use only 3 percent of their patents.[40] The rest sit on company shelves like "Rembrandts in the attic" (to echo the title of a book on the failure of companies to capitalize on their patents).[41]

Savvy CEOs are attempting to unleash the hidden value represented by their intellectual property. As Richard Homan, CEO of Xerox, put it, "My focus is on intellectual property. I'm convinced that the management of intellectual property is how value added is going to be created at Xerox. And not just here, either. Increasingly, companies that are good at managing IP will win. The ones that aren't will lose."[42] Given this sense of direction, attorneys are developing a new mindset. According to Suzanne Harrison, coauthor of the book *Edison in the Boardroom*, while attorneys must continue to "take the legal view and protect [intellectual assets], they should also be looking beyond that to find ways to use IP to generate revenue."[43] Xerox attorney Barry Smith puts it more bluntly when he describes his new job as thinking "about intellectual property as a moneymaker."[44]

With this mindset, options for creating value include licensing or selling intellectual property and creating joint ventures with companies that can maximize the value of intellectual property. The results have been dramatic at companies that have embraced an intellectual property strategy. The leader in leveraging its intellectual property is IBM, where annual patent royalties grew from $30 million in 1990 to almost $1 billion a decade later.[45]

Underscoring the relationship between intellectual property strategy and competitive advantage, attorney Victor Siber—one of the developers of IBM's intellectual property strategy—notes, "When a company makes a billion on licensing fees that money goes right to the bottom line—and it's usually money that comes from the competitors."[46]

The Quality of Your Law Department
The importance of law in gaining competitive advantage has resulted in newfound respect for the law department. As Jack Foltz, vice president and general counsel of the Sun Company, puts it: "I remember a time when I would walk into a room full of engineers, accountants, and marketers and they would look at me as if I was their daughter's first date. That no longer happens. Admit it or not, they know that when the in-house counsel arrives on the scene, he or she is not there to be a nay sayer but to help them strike a balance between business initiatives and the law."[47] A survey of *Fortune* 500 CEOs conducted by Heidrick & Struggles in 2000 confirmed this observation, concluding that the general counsel's adviser role dominates the other two roles (legal and managerial) and a key skill in serving as an adviser is the ability "to accomplish business strategies and objectives."[48]

The key role that corporate attorneys play in your business success makes it imperative that you have a set of criteria for evaluating and developing the law department. The benchmark is General Electric. The world's most respected company has the world's most respected law department. Although most of the public glory for GE's success goes to former CEO Jack Welch, a key player for Welch is Ben Heineman, the fourth-highest-paid officer at GE and leader of the 775-member law department. As Maura Smith, general counsel for Owens Corning, observes, "I've adopted the GE style of being bold, and fast, and creative. Sometimes when I get stuck, I think, 'What would Ben do?'"[49]

The following questions, drawn from a list of the GE law department's best practices, can serve as a checklist when you review your law department.[50]

- *Are you hiring the best talent?* Heineman exemplifies the legal talent in GE's law department. His accomplishments before the age of forty: graduate of Harvard College and Yale Law School (where he was editor-in-chief of the *Law Journal*), clerk to Justice Potter Stewart of the U.S. Supreme Court, and managing partner of the prestigious Washington law firm Sidley and Austin. Retaining lawyers of this caliber requires an attractive stock options package in addition to competitive salaries.
- *Are your attorneys focused on business strategy?* Heineman, who doesn't want his legal staff "stuck in a legal ghetto," has assigned each attorney to one of GE's thirteen divisions. According to one GE attorney, "GE is like a graduate school in business."[51]
- *Are your lawyers well trained?* Using a model inspired by GE's famed Crotonville training center, Heineman established the Advanced Business Course for Lawyers, which is taught by experts from GE and business schools.
- *Does your law department maximize its use of technology?* Like other functions within GE, the law department does its work on-line, with an intranet that includes a "knowledge bank" that avoids replication of work.
- *Does your law department control its budget?* Despite the company's size, GE's legal costs as a percentage of revenue are lower than the national median. A key factor in budget control at GE is an early dispute resolution program that attempts to resolve litigation by settlement, mediation, or arbitration.

If you can answer yes to these questions, you have access to a law department that will enable you to achieve competitive advantage. The mission of this twenty-first century department, as summarized by the *Corporate Counsel* LD21 committee of prominent corporate counsel in Exhibit 5.1, reflects the themes in this chapter and throughout the book.

■ Management Tools for Addressing Business/Legal Problems

Although the law plays an important role in achieving competitive advantage, your corporate attorneys should not make business decisions for you. Law is just one of myriad concerns that must be factored into your decisions. Business decisions made entirely from a legal perspective, which tends to be risk averse, might not produce the results that your shareholders expect in an entrepreneurial business world.

Your dilemma is that, in making business decisions, you must deal with the considerable complexity and uncertainty inherent in the law. This section will first describe a management tool called *decision tree analysis* that is especially useful in business/legal decision making. In fact, this tool is recommended

---

Exhibit 5.1. The Law Department Mission.

- Serving as gateways, rather than gatekeepers, law departments will function proactively to bring legal and risk consideration issues into business strategy discussions.
- Lawyers will be members of division and corporate management committees who add value by focusing attention on business opportunities made possible by changes in laws and regulations.
- Law departments will provide on-line resources that enable all employees to understand how to comply with laws and regulations and manage legal risk.
- Law departments will focus on helping companies harvest greater value from intellectual property.

Source: Stephen E. Nowlan, "Gatekeeper to Gateway," *LD21* (Spring 2001): p. 3. Copyright © 2001 NLP IP Company. Used by permission. All rights reserved.

for use when you are faced with a complex decision that relates to any aspect of your business. Following the discussion of decision tree analysis, a more specific set of tools, collectively called "alternative dispute resolution," will be reviewed, along with the importance of systems design.

Decision Tree Analysis

Earlier in this chapter, I discussed the use of intellectual property law to attack competitors who infringe on your intellectual property rights. Assume that you manage a small software company.[52] After licensing your software to another company, you discover that the licensee has violated the licensing agreement by producing its own version of your software. You bring suit, expecting to win $6 million in damages, after deducting $300,000 for legal expenses. The licensee has just offered you $1.5 million to settle the case.

In making a management decision whether to settle the case, you ask your corporate attorney to provide an analysis of your chances for success if you reject the settlement and proceed to trial. The attorney advises you that the key questions in the litigation are the following:

- Is the licensee's software substantially similar to your software? The attorney advises you that your chances of success on this issue are better than even.
- Did the licensee have access to your software before developing its software? The attorney thinks that it is likely that you will prevail on this issue.
- Is your copyright on the software valid? The attorney thinks it highly probable that the court will decide that it is.

Given this analysis, would you settle for $1.5 million or risk $300,000 by going to trial in an attempt to recover $6 million? In making this decision, you will want to answer two questions.

First, what are your overall chances for success if you go to trial? Second, can a value be placed on the litigation, given the uncertainty of winning at trial? Unfortunately, it is difficult to answer these questions based on your attorney's analysis. For instance, in an exercise similar to this case that I have used with hundreds of managers and MBA students, their estimates of overall chances for success range from 10 percent to 95 percent.

Decision tree analysis involves a three-step process in which you build a model of your decision. This model enables you to determine both the likelihood of winning at trial and the value of the litigation. The first step is to draw a diagram of the decision in the form of a tree on its side. This diagram enables you to visualize and distinguish events that can be controlled (decisions) from uncertain events. As Figure 5.3 illustrates, squares are used to represent decisions (in this case, your decision whether to continue litigating or to accept the settlement offer) and circles are used to depict uncertain events (here, the issues that must be decided in court).

The second step in building a model of the decision is to assign values to the endpoints of each branch on the tree. The "win" endpoint in Figure 5.4 has a value of $6 million, while the "lose" endpoints have a negative $300,000 value. Although not depicted on this tree, circles and additional branches could be added at other "win" endpoints to reflect the uncertainty of the amount of damages that the court will award.

The third step is to assign probabilities for each uncertain event. This requires conversion of the attorney's verbal statements to numbers. In this case, we assume that the attorney tells you that the "better than even" statement regarding the similarity issue means a 60 percent chance of success. The "it is likely" statement regarding the access issue means a 70 percent chance of success and the "highly probable" statement regarding copyright validity means an 80 percent chance of success. The decision tree in Figure 5.4 includes these probabilities.

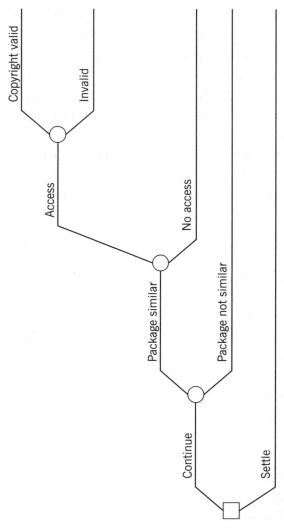

Figure 5.3. Decision Tree Diagram.

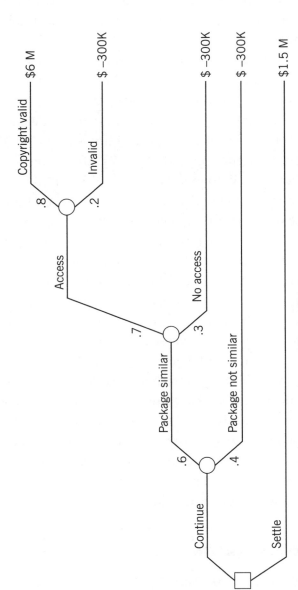

Figure 5.4. Decision Tree with Endpoint Values and Probabilities.

Copyright valid $6 M
.8
Invalid $ –300K
.2

Access

No access $ –300K
.3

Package similar
.7

.6

Package not similar $ –300K
.4

Continue

Settle $1.5 M

After developing the model in Figure 5.4, you are ready to use it to answer your questions. For instance, you can calculate the overall chance for success if you go to trial by multiplying the win probabilities along the "win" path. As Figure 5.5 shows, there is a 34 percent chance that you will be successful at trial. Furthermore, you can calculate the value of the litigation by "folding back" the tree. This requires calculating a weighted average for each uncertain event, moving from right to left. For example, the weighted average of the copyright validity issue is $4.7 million, the sum of .8 × $6 million and .2 × −$300,000. The end result shown in Figure 5.5 is an expected value of $1.8 million. Thus, if you "played the averages," you would continue with the litigation because this amount is greater than the settlement offer.

The decision tree is a powerful tool that enables you to make a number of management decisions relating to legal issues, such as how to maximize the use of limited financial resources and how much to pay expert witnesses who could improve your chances for success. But even if you stop at Step 1 and don't use the model for quantitative analyses, the picture of the decision in decision tree form is useful when discussing complex, multi-issue matters with your attorney. Decision trees can be used for a variety of legal decisions beyond settlement decisions, such as a decision whether to proceed with a merger, and are also useful when dealing with marketing, finance, operations, and other matters beyond the law that involve complexity and uncertainty. Commercial software produced by Vanguard, TreeAge, and other companies simplifies the use of decision tree analysis by managers.

Alternative Dispute Resolution

Alternative dispute resolution (ADR) involves the search for alternatives to litigation in resolving disputes. As noted previously, GE's early dispute resolution program is an important factor in its budget management. According to Brackett Denniston, GE's

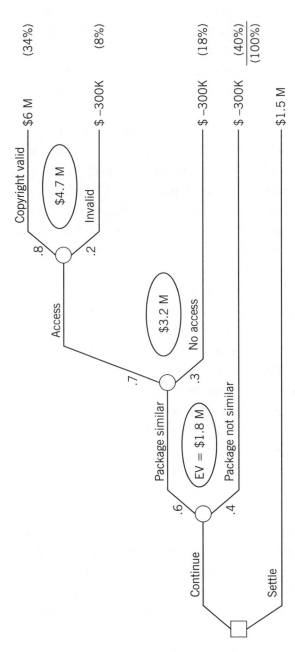

Figure 5.5. Overall Probability of Success and Expected Values.

senior litigation counsel, ADR has saved "millions of dollars" for the company.[53] Other companies also recognize that traditional litigation might not be the most cost-effective process for resolving disputes. Because of its impact in reducing legal costs, ADR might have another meaning within law firms: "alarming drop in revenue."[54]

In addition to legal costs, managers incur significant opportunity costs when they are involved in litigation. Studies show that in a mid-sized company, "the disruption factor of a typical patent infringement case amounts to the loss of about six to eight months of new product development."[55]

ADR is built on two basic models, mediation and arbitration, that involve the assistance of a neutral third party. A key difference between the two processes is that in a mediation the third party is not authorized to decide the dispute. Mediation is, in effect, a negotiation between the disputing parties assisted by the third party. As in traditional litigation, a third-party arbitrator is authorized to make a decision. Arbitration decisions are typically binding on the parties, although it is possible to ask the arbitrator for a non-binding decision. Unlike litigation, arbitration gives the parties in the process the right to select the third party, allows them to avoid publicity, and may substantially lower their costs.

The mini-trial illustrates an effective ADR procedure developed from the mediation model. In the first mini-trial, Telecredit sued TRW for $6 million, claiming patent infringement.[56] For almost three years, the case had languished in the court system, the two companies exchanged around a hundred thousand documents and spent close to $500,000 in legal fees. After realizing that their legal costs would continue to mount over the next several years, they developed an out-of-court "mini-trial" process to resolve their dispute.

During the mini-trial, attorneys for each side presented their case to two executives, the president of Telecredit and the vice-president of TRW, both of whom had authority to settle the case. A neutral party (a retired judge who was an expert on patent law) moderated the process. Following the presentations, the two executives met for thirty minutes and resolved the dispute. Among the benefits of this mini-trial: (1) an opportunity for each executive to hear the case as presented by the opposing attorney, (2) an estimated $1 million savings in legal fees, and (3) a chance to resolve the dispute in a manner that preserved the business relationship between the companies, as opposed to the win-lose scenario that characterizes litigation.

Three key tools are available for management use in implementing ADR: policy statements, suitability screens, and contract clauses.

An ADR Policy Statement

In the intellectual property scenario that was used earlier in this chapter to illustrate decision tree analysis, the defendant offered to settle the case for $1.5 million. In working with managers, I have discovered that their typical reaction to a settlement offer like this is that the person who offered settlement must have a weak case. Research has shown that most people "reactively devalue" proposals simply because they are made by the other side.[57] An ADR policy statement is an important tool for avoiding reactive devaluation—if a company is on record as preferring to avoid litigation, it can make such an offer without undercutting its own position. The best-known statement, developed by the CPR Institute for Dispute Resolution and adopted by over four thousand operating companies, is shown in Exhibit 5.2.

Suitability Screens

Companies like GE and Xerox have developed suitability screens, which are checklists used to determine whether mediation, arbitration, or litigation is suitable for use in resolving a particular dispute. These checklists include factors such as the business

□

Exhibit 5.2. ADR Policy Statement.

We recognize that for many disputes there is a less expensive, more effective method of resolution than the traditional lawsuit. Alternative dispute resolution (ADR) procedures involve collaborative techniques which can often spare businesses the high costs of litigation.

In recognition of the foregoing, we subscribe to the following statements of principle on behalf of company and its domestic subsidiaries:

In the event of a business dispute between our company and another company which has made or will then make a similar statement, we are prepared to explore with that other party resolution of the dispute through negotiation or ADR techniques before pursuing full-scale litigation. If either party believes that that dispute is not suitable for ADR techniques, or if such techniques do not produce results satisfactory to the disputants, either party may proceed with litigation.

CHIEF EXECUTIVE OFFICER   _____

CHIEF LEGAL OFFICER   _____

DATE   _____

Source: Copyright © 2001 CPR Institute for Dispute Resolution, 366 Madison Avenue, New York, NY 10017–3122; (212) 949-6490, http://www.cpradr.org. Reprinted with permission of CPR Institute.

Note: The CPR Institute is a nonprofit initiative of five hundred general counsels of major corporations, leading law firms, and prominent legal academics whose mission is to install alternative dispute resolution (ADR) into the mainstream of legal practice.

relationship between the companies, the effect of negative publicity, the effect on other cases, the nature of the legal and factual issues, the amount of damages at stake, and the legal costs.[58]

Contract Clauses

Your attorney should be able to provide you with contract clauses for use in negotiation. For example, you might negotiate separate contract clauses for mediation or arbitration, or you might use a step approach. A *step approach* is an agreement stating that the disputing companies will first try to settle a dispute by negotiation and, if that fails, will move to mediation. If mediation is unsuccessful, the case goes to binding arbitration.[59]

Law departments at many companies have embraced the use of some or all of these dispute resolution tools to encourage the use of ADR. What is still needed, however, is a trip to the balcony to gain perspective on how the individual pieces fit together as a dispute resolution system. The dispute resolution system depicted in Figure 5.6 is generic. Moving from left to right, the starting point is a company-wide policy statement similar to the one in Exhibit 5.2. The system includes two suitability screens for use during contract negotiations or, if there is no ADR clause in a contract, after a dispute arises. The first screen helps you decide whether to use binding or non-binding processes and the second enables you to select one of the two binding process, litigation or binding arbitration.

The non-binding path embodies several fundamental principles of systems design.[60] For instance, you should start with the options that are lower in cost and give the disputing parties more control. These options also enable the parties to develop a resolution to the dispute that builds on their interests, as opposed to litigation or binding arbitration, which focus on who is "right" in a legal sense. And the system includes loopbacks. For instance, after receiving a non-binding decision from an arbitrator, the parties can loop back to negotiation or mediation.

Dispute resolution represents a specific type of contract negotiation. You should also consider your approach in reviewing contract negotiations in general. Too often, companies focus on the results of a negotiation (Did we make a deal? How much did we pay?) and do not review the manner in which the negotiation was conducted (for instance, Did we try to craft an agreement that satisfies the interests of the other side, as well as our own interests?).[61]

A focus on contract results can harm relationships with your suppliers and customers. For instance, a major reason for

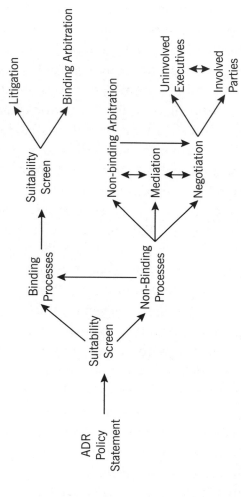

Figure 5.6. Dispute Resolution System.

the success of the DuPont Legal Model is that, rather than simply forcing cost reductions on outside law firms (a result that might look impressive in the short term), the DuPont law department developed a solution that takes into account the interests of the outside law firms.

■ Competitive Advantage Through an Ethical Corporate Culture

Does business ethics pay? Does an ethical corporate culture create competitive advantage? Studies have determined that these questions are difficult to answer because of problems in deciding whether one company is more ethical than another and whether a company's profitability is a result of ethical conduct or other factors. Nevertheless, a survey of academic studies published in 1999 concluded, "33 studies showed a positive link between corporate ethics and profit, 14 showed no effect or were inconclusive and only five suggested a negative relationship."[62]

It is logical that an ethical corporate culture creates an environment that is conducive to gaining competitive advantage. As Harvard professor Lynn Paine notes, "the economic case for corporate ethics has both a negative and a positive aspect. . . . The negative case for ethics focuses on risk management and cost avoidance, [and] the positive case emphasizes innovation, productivity gains, and revenue enhancement."[63]

An example of the cost avoidance case for ethical business behavior is the $340 million fine that Daiwa Bank had to pay for its delay in disclosing over $1 billion in losses as a result of unauthorized trading by one of its employees.[64] The positive aspect of corporate ethics is illustrated by findings reported in KPMG's *2000 Organizational Integrity Survey*.[65] The survey concluded that a commitment to business integrity helps companies attract and retain loyal employees and customers. For instance, among employees who felt that their management acted ethically, 81 percent would recommend their companies to recruits and 80 percent believe that their customers would recommend their companies to others. Among employees who felt that their management did not act ethically, the percentages dropped to 21 percent and 40 percent respectively.

Recognizing the link between an ethical culture and competitive advantage, most companies have embraced business ethics management over the past decade. A 1999 London Business School/Arthur Andersen survey concluded that close to 80 percent of companies use Codes of Conduct and that: "Existing business ethics activities are perceived to improve business performance, *not* hinder it. . . . This outcome makes a strong case for business ethics programmes as creators of competitive advantage."[66]

Research on ethics programs frequently distinguishes between a compliance approach and an integrity approach.[67] The compliance approach is said to be lawyer-driven, with an emphasis on preventing legal liability. The integrity approach is said to be management driven, with a goal of encouraging responsible conduct that extends beyond avoiding liability.[68] Although the compliance approach predominates over the integrity approach,[69] Professor Paine forcefully argues for an integrity approach, noting that "legal compliance is unlikely to unleash much moral imagination or commitment."[70] As noted by former Securities and Exchange Commission chairman Richard Breeden, "It is not an adequate ethical standard to aspire to get through the day without being indicted."[71]

While there may be a theoretical distinction between compliance and integrity approaches, studies have shown that in practice ethics programs are not teeter-totters, where companies must adopt either a compliance approach or an integrity approach. Many companies combine both approaches.[72] According to William Lytton, general counsel for International Paper, compliance is "more than just obeying the law. It's 'Let's do the right thing.' Now compliance is a subset of ethics."[73]

Using the Manager's Legal Plan to Link Law, Ethics, and Profits

Despite the common use of codes of conduct, there is disturbing evidence that current employee ethics programs are not successful. The Association of Certified Fraud Examiners estimates that U.S. organizations lose $400 billion each year as a result of their employees' criminal or unethical behavior.[74] U.S. stores lose over $2 billion more annually through employee theft than they do through shoplifting.[75] And the KPMG 2000 survey concluded that 76 percent of employees have observed violations of company standards or the law over the past year. Around 50 percent of employees believe that the misconduct is serious enough to cause their organizations to "significantly lose public trust."[76]

Clearly there is a disconnect within many organizations between the company's code of conduct and actual conduct in the workplace. A possible reason for this disconnect is that, by focusing on law and ethics in developing and implementing their codes, companies overlook profits, a third force that is the end result of competitive advantage and a key component of a free society. Professor Tim Fort of the University of Michigan Business School has developed a three-part ethical context for business decisions that draws on the works of philosophers from a variety disciplines, including William Frederick, Michael Novak, and F. A. Hayek.[77] As illustrated in Figure 5.7, the three parts are ethics, law, and profits.

Most companies, whether using a compliance approach or an integrity approach, focus on the law and ethics points of the triangle and ignore the influence of profits. For instance, the 1999 London Business School/Arthur Andersen survey included a list of the factors that influence business ethics activities. The list is dominated by factors such as the desire to protect or improve

Figure 5.7. **The Ethical Context for Business Decisions.**

reputation and the need to meet corporate governance guidelines. Profits and competitive advantage are not mentioned.[78]

Studies have emphasized the importance of corporate culture in ethics management: "To achieve desired outcomes, concerns for ethics and legal compliance must be baked into the culture of the organization."[79] In other words, "executives cannot just descend from some ethical mountaintop with a couple of stone tablets and expect immediate compliance."[80] Yet that is exactly the impression that many employees have when ethics programs focus on the first two points on the triangle while ignoring the third.

What process can managers use to incorporate the third point of the triangle, the profit motive, into business ethics management? The Manager's Legal Plan, with its emphasis on moving to the balcony to transform legal problems into business problems, is a useful tool in accomplishing this goal. Exhibit 5.3 provides examples of this transformation, drawn from earlier chapters. For example, what starts as a legal concern, such as reducing workers' compensation costs, is transformed into a broad business concern, in this case encouraging safety at home as well as at work. This emphasis on safety reflects a high-level ethical standard—concern for the well-being of others. In the words of the head of a DuPont strategic business unit, "I place a high value

Exhibit 5.3. Reframing Legal Concerns as Business Concerns.

Legal Concerns	Business Concerns
Product Liability	Develop products that meet customer needs.
Workers' Compensation	Encourage safety at work and at home.
Wrongful Discharge	Emphasize honesty in all communications with or about employees.
Sexual Harassment	Remove barriers that prevent employees from focusing on customer needs.
Environmental Regulation	Meet customer needs while preserving the environment for future generations.

on the tradition of viewing safety as 'caring for people. . . .' Caring for people means caring for all of our people . . . all of the time. It doesn't matter if the person is a company employee or a contract worker. And it doesn't matter if the safety risk is on the job or in the home."[81]

The business concerns listed in Exhibit 5.3 dovetail with the subjects addressed in corporate codes of conduct: safe products for customers, workplace safety, honesty, diversity, and environmental protection. By using the Manager's Legal Plan to address these concerns not merely as ethical values or legal requirements but instead as a source of competitive advantage, you have an opportunity to "bake them into the culture" in a manner that allows your employees to understand their importance in economic terms.

Dispute Prevention

In closing this section on values, one value deserves special mention because of its role in guiding your interaction with company lawyers as you work together on legal matters. This value is dispute prevention. *Dispute prevention* is a term that has been used for many years with a variety of meanings. Only in recent years has the meaning crystallized into a guide for management conduct: "It is often more important to predict what people will do than to predict what a court will do. . . . Winning a lawsuit can be ruinous."[82] As Voltaire reputedly put it, "I was never ruined but twice: once when I lost a lawsuit, and once when I won one."

The dispute prevention philosophy tracks closely themes that are emphasized in the best-selling management book of all time, *In Search of Excellence:*[83] stay close to your customers and be obsessed with service and quality. These themes, which lie at the heart of quality programs, are especially important in today's market-driven, customer-focused world.

I once stayed at a Marriott hotel the night before I was scheduled to give an early morning corporate presentation. I asked the front desk for a wake-up call, which I never received. Fortunately, I had set an alarm clock and arrived for my presentation on time. But I recalled reading in *In Search of Excellence* that the Marriott CEO personally reads every complaint and I decided to test the system. For the only time in my life, I filled out a hotel complaint card, noting the problem with the wake-up call. Three weeks later, I received the letter in Exhibit 5.4 from the president of Marriott. What had been an unpleasant experience was transformed into a pleasant memory of a CEO who cared enough about customers to respond to their complaints (even though my last name is misspelled in the letter).

Contrast this example with a recent case involving a major utility company. A company lineman removed a fuse from a transformer box, which turned off a traffic signal. A few minutes later, two cars collided at the intersection, resulting in the death of the twelve-year-old daughter of one of the drivers.

Apparently the company took a traditional approach to the accident, which is to focus on legal rights in court, rather than on the feelings of the victim's parents. In a newspaper article

Exhibit 5.4. Letter from Marriott President.

corporation

| INTERNATIONAL | Marriott Drive | J. Willard Marriott, Jr. |
| HEADQUARTERS | Washington, D.C. 20058 | President |

Mr. George Seidel
76 Peter Coutts Circle
Stanford, California 94305

Dear Mr. Seidel:

It was truly disappointing to learn about the problem you had
with our wake-up service. Please accept my sincere apologies.

I have forwarded your comments to our Dallas/Ft. Worth Airport
Marriott and I have asked our General Manager to give prompt
attention to the matter.

Thank you for taking the time to write. I hope you will allow
us another opportunity to serve you soon so that we may regain
your complete confidence.

Sincerely,

J. W. Marriott, Jr.

about the accident, a company representative stated that the company owed no duty to warn that the traffic light wasn't working. The company's main duty, he said, was "to protect its own workers." The article went on to point out that the executive "expressed no sympathy for the accident victim."[84]

According to one expert, "The single greatest cause for adverse litigation is when the victims feel the company doesn't really care."[85] The father of the victim in this case, upset after reading the comments of the company representative, decided to sue the company. Even then, the utility company attorney did not express regret over the daughter's death. When the case proceeded to trial, the parents' attorney asked the jury for $10 million in damages. The end result: an award of $37 million, $17 million for the decedent's father and $20 million for her mother.

Although the company may eventually win on appeal, the case provides a lesson in the philosophy that should touch every aspect of your attempt to use law for competitive advantage. As stated earlier, this philosophy focuses more on what people will do than on what a court will do. The Russian author Alexander Solzhenitsyn once expressed the following concern about the Western world: "Whenever the tissue of life is woven of legalistic relations, there is an atmosphere of moral mediocrity, paralyzing man's noblest impulses."[86] By adopting a dispute prevention philosophy, you not only have a chance to prevent expensive litigation, you also have the opportunity to exercise a "noble impulse" by expressing genuine sympathy to those who have suffered loss or injury.

CHAPTER SUMMARY

After defining competitive advantage and noting problems with conventional management approaches to the law, Chapter One describes a plan that enables you to use the law to seize competitive advantage—the Manager's Legal Plan. Chapters Two, Three, and Four illustrate how you can use this plan to seize competitive advantage when you deal with difficult legal problems such as product liability, workers' compensation, and environmental regulation. This closing chapter examines three general concerns—legal resources, management tools, and the role of values—that will enable your company to gain competitive advantage across a broad range of legal issues.

Conventional strategies for developing and using legal resources involve two fundamental decisions: Should the company develop an in-house legal staff or rely on outside law firms? and How can the company control legal costs? In answering the first question, in-house law departments generally play a key role in creating value and providing higher perceived quality. With regard to cost control, the chapter described several alternatives to traditional hourly billing.

In focusing on these two questions, companies overlook several larger concerns. First, in a market-driven company, attorneys must focus on the external customer to provide the best advice to their internal clients. As part of their training, for example, McDonald's attorneys flip hamburgers in the company's restaurants. Second, law departments must be vigilant in using best practices developed by other functions in the company. An example is the DuPont Legal Model, which has resulted in a substantial reduction in legal costs. Third, companies should consider opportunities for law departments to become profit centers. In-house attorneys are especially well suited to lead their companies' intellectual property initiatives. The chapter also provides a checklist to use in evaluating the quality of your company's law department.

Following discussion of legal resources, the chapter turns to tools that managers can use to address business/legal problems. Decision tree analysis is an all-purpose tool that can be used to make decisions relating to law and other functional areas. In making settlement decisions, for example, decision tree analysis provides a more scientific approach than conventional decision making.

Another set of tools relates to alternative dispute resolution. ADR includes a variety of processes based on arbitration and mediation models. Conventional tools include the ADR policy statement, suitability screens, and contract templates. These tools can be incorporated into a framework using principles of systems design.

The chapter closes with an examination of the role of values in gaining competitive advantage. The conventional approach is to develop an ethics program based on a lawyer-driven compliance strategy or a management-driven integrity strategy. Despite growth in the use of corporate codes of conduct, there is evidence that ethics programs are not successful. Use of the Manager's Legal Plan provides an opportunity for companies to link values and economics in a way that creates competitive advantage.

Questions to Consider

1. Regardless of whether they work in-house or for outside law firms, are your company attorneys focused on your customers?
2. What practices used in other areas of the company, such as strategic partnering, could be adapted for use by the law department?

3. Can you turn your law department into a profit center—for example, through the sale or licensing of your intellectual property?

4. Using the five questions drawn from GE's best practices, how do you rate the quality of your law department?

5. Do you have a dispute resolution system that incorporates an ADR policy statement?

Notes

Chapter One

1. "In A New Economy, Old Issues Are The Problem, Survey Says." Available online: http://www.bus.umich.edu/current/ppi.html (September 7, 2001).
2. Michael A. Hitt, R. Duane Ireland, and Robert E. Hoskisson, *Strategic Management: Competitiveness and Globalization,* 2nd ed. (St. Paul, MN: West, 1997), p. 91.
3. Thomas D. Cavenagh, *Business Dispute Resolution* (Cincinnati, OH: West Legal Studies in Business, 2000), p. 84.
4. George J. Siedel, "Six Forces and the Legal Environment of Business: The Relative Value of Business Law Among Business School Core Courses," *American Business Law Journal* 37 (2000): 727.
5. Siedel, "Six Forces," p. 728.
6. Michael Porter, *Competitive Advantage* (New York: Free Press, 1985), p. 3.
7. Porter, *Competitive Advantage,* p. 3.
8. Charles Gasparino, "Merrill Is Paying in Wake of Analysts' Call on Tech Stock," *Wall Street Journal* (July 20, 2001): C1.
9. Leigh Thompson, *The Mind and Heart of the Negotiator* (Upper Saddle River, NJ: Prentice Hall, 1998), pp. 215–219.

10. *Booth* v. *Mary Carter Paint Co.,* 202 So.2d 8 (1967). Although the decision was overruled by the Florida Supreme Court in *Ward* v. *Ochoa,* 284 So.2d 385 (1977), the name "Mary Carter" agreement has survived.

11. *Judas Priest* v. *Second Judicial District,* 760 P.2d 137 (1988).

12. "No, California, There Is No Santa," *Economist* (May 13, 1989): 33.

13. Ashlea Ebeling, "Sue Everywhere," *Forbes* (October 16, 2000): 128.

14. Frank A. Piantidosi and Michael Murphey, "International Corruption: Finally U.S. Companies Get a Break," *Corporate Counsel* (October, 1999): A18.

15. William Glaberson, "U.S. Courts Become Arbiters of Global Rights and Wrongs," *New York Times* (June 21, 2001): A1.

16. Mark Curriden, "Putting the Squeeze on Juries," *ABA Journal* (August 2000): 53.

17. Michael J. Patrick, "E-Mail Data Is a Ticking Time Bomb," *National Law Journal* (December 20, 1993): 14.

18. Thompson, *Mind and Heart of the Negotiator,* p. 227.

19. "Are Efforts to Extend Patent and Copyright Laws Good for Business or Good for Society?" *Knowledge @ Wharton.* Available online: http://knowledge.wharton.upenn.edu/ (September 6, 2001).

20. Karl E. Weick, *Sensemaking in Organizations* (Thousand Oaks, CA: Sage, 1995), pp. 54–55.

21. Weick, *Sensemaking,* p. 55.

22. "Benjamin W. Heineman Jr.," *ACCA DOCKET* (Fall, 1994): 26.

23. "In-House Counsel for the 21st Century," American Corporate Counsel Association. Available online: http://www.acca.com/Surveys/CEO/control.html (September 7, 2001).

24. J. Edward Russo and Paul J. H. Schoemaker, *Decision Traps* (New York: Fireside, 1990): Chapters 3 and 4.

25. William Ury, *Getting Past No* (New York: Bantam Books, 1993), p. 38.

Chapter Two

1. "Still Killing," *Economist* (August 19, 2000): 55.

2. Bernard Wysocki, "Manufacturers Are Hit with More Lawsuits, Rising Insurance Costs," *Wall Street Journal* (June 3, 1976): A1.

3. Jill Andresky, "A World Without Insurance?" *Forbes* (July 15, 1985): 42.
4. David Zeman and Janet L. Fix, "When Secrecy Explodes," *Detroit Free Press* (July 7, 2000): 1A.
5. Jerry Geisel, "Gun Firm Pays $6.8 Million to Attorney," *Business Insurance* (November 13, 1978): 12.
6. Peter Fritsch and Jose De Cordoba, "An Attorney Switches Sides After Car Crash; Now Ford Is the Enemy," *Wall Street Journal* (August 31, 2000): A1.
7. E. Patrick McGuire, *The Impact of Product Liability* (New York: Conference Board, 1988), pp. 6, 8.
8. "Tortuous Reform," *Economist* (March 30, 1996): 20.
9. *Banks* v. *ICI,* 450 S.E.2d 671 (1994).
10. W. Page Keeton, Dan B. Dobbs, Robert E. Keeton, and David G. Owen, *Prosser and Keeton on the Law of Torts* (St. Paul, MN: West, 1984), p. 693.
11. Michael Edgerton, "How One Firm Learned Its Lesson in Liability Cases," *Detroit Free Press* (March 19, 1978): D1.
12. "Sports Company Tackles Product Liability Reform by Working with Other Companies, Organizations," *Focus* (December 1993): 2.
13. Ronald Bailey, "Legal Mayhem," *Forbes* (November 14, 1988): 97.
14. Spencer Abraham, "American Injustice: The Case for Legal Reform," *Imprimis* (September 1997): 2.
15. *Cipollone* v. *Liggett Group, Inc.,* 112 S. Ct. 2608 (1992).
16. Timothy Aeppel, "Goodyear Wins Round in Suit over Warranty," *Wall Street Journal* (February 8, 2000): B5.
17. *Bravman* v. *Baxter Healthcare Corporation,* 984 F.2d 71 (1993).
18. David MacIntosh, "What Is Product Liability?" *International Business Lawyer* (February 1998): 53.
19. Craig S. Smith, "Chinese Discover Product-Liability Suits," *Wall Street Journal* (November 13, 1997): B1.
20. *Anderson* v. *Associated Grocers, Inc.,* 525 P.2d 284 (1974).
21. Milo Geyelin, "Yes, $145 Billion Deals Tobacco a Huge Blow, But Not a Killing One," *Wall Street Journal* (July 17, 2000): A8.
22. Dow Chemical Company, *Annual Report* (1998), p. 53.
23. Richard Greene, "Peeking Beneath the Corporate Veil," *Forbes* (August 13, 1984): 58.

24. *Uniroyal* v. *Martinez,* 977 S.W.2d 328 (1998).
25. Virginia I. Postrel, "The Lessons of Email Deceit," *Forbes ASAP* (October 6, 1997): 24.
26. *Green* v. *Ford Motor Company,* 742 P.2d 639 (1987).
27. H. C. Barksdale (ed.), *Marketing in Progress* (Austin, TX: Holt, Rinehart and Winston, 1964), p. 199.

Chapter Three

1. Commission on the Future of Worker-Management Relations, *Fact Finding Report* (Washington, DC: U.S. Department of Labor and U.S. Department of Commerce, 1994), p. 134.
2. Mark D. Fefer, "What to Do About Workers' Comp," *Fortune* (June 29, 1992): 80; Stephen D. Solomon, "Keeping in Touch," *Inc.* (February, 1990): 100.
3. Sarah Grabill, "Unintentional Injuries Are Among Leading Causes of Death in the U.S.," National Safety Council. Available online: http://www.nsc.org/news/nrrptinj.htm (September 10, 2001).
4. Bureau of Labor Statistics, "Census of Fatal Occupational Injuries Summary." Available online: http://stats.bls.gov/news.release/cfoi.nr0.htm (September 10, 2001).
5. Roman F. Diekemper, "Controlling Workers' Compensation Costs," *Public Utilities Fortnightly* (February 15, 1992): 26.
6. Mark D. Fefer, "Taking Control of Your Workers' Comp Costs," *Fortune* (October 3, 1994): 131.
7. U.S. Postal Service, *Annual Report* (1998), p. 41.
8. Diekemper, "Controlling Workers' Compensation Costs," p. 26.
9. "An Overview of Workers' Compensation Systems in Nine Highly Developed Nations," *NCCI Digest* (December 1993): 67.
10. W. Page Keeton, Dan B. Dobbs, Robert E. Keeton, and David G. Owen, *Prosser and Keeton on the Law of Torts* (St. Paul, MN: West, 1984), p. 573.
11. See, for example, Texas Workers' Compensation Commission, "Injured Worker Rights and Responsibilities." Available online: http://www.twcc.state.tx.us/information/workerrights.html (September 10, 2001).

12. *Gacioch* v. *Stroh Brewery Co.,* 466 N.W.2d 302 (1990); *Gacioch* v. *Stroh Brewery Co.,* 396 N.W.2d 1 (1986).
13. *DeNardo* v. *Fairmount Foundries Cranston, Inc.,* 399 A.2d 1229, 1237 (1979).
14. Lawrence D. Sukay, "Safety Programs Alone Don't Work in Reducing Workers' Compensation Costs," *Risk Management* (September 1993): 46.
15. *Wolfe* v. *Sibley,* 330 N.E.2d 603, 605 (1975).
16. *Friedman* v. *NBC,* 577 N.Y.S. 2d 517 (1991).
17. Eugene Carlson, "States' Widely Varying Laws on Disability Costs Irk Firms," *Wall Street Journal* (October 11, 1983): 37.
18. Jim Carlton, "California Law Alters Workers' Compensation," *Wall Street Journal* (July 19, 1993): A2.
19. American Insurance Association, *Success Stories: State Efforts to Reform Workers' Compensation Laws* (Washington, DC: American Insurance Association, 1996), pp. 3–5.
20. *Beauchesne* v. *David London* & *Co.,* 375 A.2d 920 (1977).
21. "Curiosity Doesn't Pay," *American Bar Association Journal* (August 1984): 178.
22. Mark Rust, "New Tactics for Injured Workers," *ABA Journal* (October 1, 1987): 73.
23. Ty Hutchison, "Adding Insult to Injury," *Small Business Reports* (February 1994): 43.
24. Brent Winans and Gregory Cairns, "Reducing Workers' Compensation Claims," *Risk Management* (October 1996): 31–34, 36.
25. "Getting to the Root of the Problem—The Importance of Incident Investigation," *Executive Safety News* (1998). Available online: http://www.dupont.com/safety/esn98–1/incinv.html (September 10, 2001).
26. *DSM Responsible Care Progress Report* (Heerlen, The Netherlands: DSM, 1996), pp. 22, 63.
27. Linda Himelstein, "The Asbestos Case of the 1990s?" *Business Week* (January 16, 1995): 82.
28. Michele Galen, "Repetitive Stress: The Pain Has Just Begun," *Business Week* (July 13, 1992): 142.
29. "Few Companies Are Using Ergonomics Programs . . . Yet," *HR Focus* (August 2000): 8.

30. Robert H. Sand, "Firestone Wins an Ergonomics Battle; BP Loses an Employee Suit for Punitive Damages," *Employee Relations Law Journal* 21 (1995): 139–142.

31. Ellen Newborne, "Workers in Pain: Employees Up In Arms," *USA Today* (January 9, 1997): 2B.

32. Solomon, "Keeping in Touch," p. 101.

33. "Labor Letter," *Wall Street Journal* (September 22, 1992): 1.

34. Solomon, "Keeping in Touch," p. 101.

35. Sukay, "Safety Programs Alone Don't Work in Reducing Workers' Compensation Costs," p. 44.

36. Mark Carter, "Workers' Comp Derailment: Expectations Not Met," *Risk Management* (May 1991): 26.

37. Shirley Musich, Deborah Napier, and D. W. Edington, "The Association of Health Risks with Workers' Compensation Costs," *Journal of Occupational and Environmental Medicine* 43 (2001): 534.

38. Marilyn Chase, "Healthy Assets," *Wall Street Journal* (May 1, 2000): R9.

39. "Tate & Lyle Sees Sweet Rewards of Safety," *Executive Safety News* (2000). Available online: http://www.dupont.com/safety/esn00–2/tatelyle.html (October 4, 2001).

40. "Encourage Your Employees to Take Something Home from Work—Safety," *Executive Safety News* (1997). Available online: http://www.dupont.com/safety/esn97–4/encemp.html (October 4, 2001).

41. James D. Blinn and Pamela J. Saunders, "The Net Benefit of Disability Integration," *Risk Management* (December 1995): 30.

42. Brian V. Kelley, "Health and Savings: Integrated Disability Management," *Risk Management* (November 1999): 24.

43. "Cigna Integrated Care Overview." Available online: http://www.cigna.com/newsroom/background/f971000.html (September 24, 2000).

44. Jeremy Main, "When Accidents Don't Happen," *Fortune* (September 6, 1982): 68.

45. Jackson Lewis, "Workplace 2000," *Interchange* (Spring 2000): 1–2.

46. James A. Burns, "Use and Abuse of Performance Appraisals," *Employee Relations Law Journal* 22 (1996): 167.

47. Lucinda A. Low, Patrick M. Norton, and Daniel M. Drory (eds.), *The International Lawyer's Deskbook* (Chicago: American Bar Association, 1996), p. 352.

48. *Toussaint* v. *Blue Cross & Blue Shield,* 292 N.W.2d 880 (1980).

49. *Fortune* v. *National Cash Register Company,* 364 N.E.2d 1251 (1977).

50. *Wagenseller* v. *Scottsdale Memorial Hospital,* 710 P.2d 1025 (1985).

51. *Hill* v. *Buck,* 678 S.W.2d 612 (1984).

52. Gregory Stricharchuk, "Fired Employees Turn the Reason for Dismissal into a Legal Weapon," *Wall Street Journal* (October 20, 1986): 31.

53. John Ruess, "$61 Million Awarded for Firing," *Times Tribune* (April 5, 1985): 1.

54. Marshall Sella, "More Big Bucks in Jury Verdicts," *ABA Journal* (July 1989): 70.

55. Nicholas Varchaver, "Turmoil at Triton," *American Lawyer* (March 1993): 56–58.

56. Randall Samborn, "At-Will Doctrine Under Fire," *National Law Journal* (October 14, 1991): 40.

57. Tanya A. Salgado, "References Given in Good Faith Gain Protection Across Country," *Executive Newsletter* (January 1997): 6, 8.

58. Samborn, "At-Will Doctrine Under Fire," p. 40.

59. Helene Cooper and Thomas Kamm, "Much of Europe Eases Its Rigid Labor Laws and Temps Proliferate," *Wall Street Journal* (June 4, 1998): A1.

60. Daniel Eisenberg, "Rise of the Permatemp," *Time* (July 12, 1999): 48.

61. "Companies Stop Giving References," *Fresno Bee* (June 7, 1993): C4.

62. "Libel/Slander Litigation," Susman Godfrey L.L.P. Available online: http://www.susmangodfrey.com/practice/libel.html (September 10, 2001).

63. *Zechman* v. *Merrill Lynch,* 1990 U.S., Dist. LEXIS 15949 (1990).

64. *Lewis* v. *Equitable,* 389 N.W.2d 876 (1986).

65. James N. Dertouzos and Lynn A. Karoly, *Labor Market Responses to Employer Liability* (Santa Monica, CA: Rand, 1992), pp. xi–xiv.

66. Elizabeth J. DuFresnes, "Honest Employee Evaluations: Risk Management for the 90s," *World Reports* (July-September 1994): 43.

67. "Trust in Me," *Economist* (December 16, 1995): 61.

68. Robert S. Adler and Ellen R. Peirce, "The Legal, Ethical, and Social Implications of the 'Reasonable Woman' Standard," *Fordham Law Review* 61 (1993): 803.

69. "Jury Awards UPS Manager $80.7 Million on Her Sex Bias, Retaliation Claims," *BNAC Communicator* (Summer 1998): 22.

70. Rachel Konrad, "Harassed Female Millwright Wins Suit," *Detroit Free Press* (July 20, 1999). Available online: http://www.detroitfree press.com/business/qdc20.htm (October 4, 2001).

71. "Mitsubishi Settles Record $34 Million Harassment Suit," *BNAC Communicator* (Summer 1998): 20.

72. Joann Miller, "Ford: The High Cost of Harassment," *Business Week* (November 15, 1999): 94.

73. Junda Woo, "Baker & McKenzie Is Told to Pay Punitive Damages," *Wall Street Journal* (September 2, 1994): B3.

74. *Weeks v. Baker & McKenzie,* 63 Cal. App.4th 1128 (1998).

75. Harvey Berkman, "Record USIA Deal Ends a 23-Year Saga," *National Law Journal* (April 10, 2000): A1, A10.

76. "Verdicts and Settlements," *National Law Journal* (December 27, 1999—January 3, 2000): A14-A15.

77. *Meritor Savings Bank v. Vinson,* 106 S. Ct. 2399 (1986).

78. *Meritor,* 2404–05.

79. "Sexual Harassment at the Workplace—Part Two, *EIRR* (January 1998): 28.

80. "Ruling in Malaysia on Sexual Harassment Is First of Its Kind," *Asian Wall Street Journal* (January 9, 1997): 2.

81. *Faragher v. City of Boca Raton,* 118 S. Ct. 2275, 2281 (1998).

82. *Faragher,* p. 2293.

83. David Machlowitz and Marilyn M. Machlowitz, "Preventing Sexual Harassment," *ABA Journal* (October 1, 1987): 79.

84. *Robinson v. Jacksonville Shipyards,* 760 F. Supp. 1486, 1505 (1991).

85. *Fenton v. Hisan,* 174 F.3d 827, 830 (1999).

86. Peter Aronson, "Justices' Sex Harassment Decisions Spark Fears," *National Law Journal* (November 9, 1998): A1.

87. Troy Segal, "Getting Serious About Sexual Harassment," *Business Week* (November 2, 1992): 82.

88. Michael Barrier, "Sexual Harassment," *Nation's Business* (December 1998): 17.

89. Frances A. McMorris, "Employees Face Greater Liability in Race Cases," *Wall Street Journal* (July 1, 1999): B1.

90. *Booker v. Budget Rent-A-Car Systems,* 17 F. Supp.2d 735, 743 (1998).

91. *Lockard* v. *Pizza Hut,* 162 F.3d 1062, 1067 (1998).
92. *Lockard,* p. 1074.
93. *Respect and Responsibility* (Midland, MI: Dow Chemical Company, 1999), pp. 8–9.

Chapter Four

1. Thomas N. Gladwin, "A Call for Sustainable Development," *Financial Times* (December 13, 1999 supplement): 2–4.
2. James P. Womack and Daniel T. Jones, *Lean Thinking* (London: Touchstone, 1997).
3. This example from *Lean Thinking* is described in Chapter 3 of Paul Hawken, Amory Lovins, and L. Hunter Lovins, *Natural Capitalism: Creating the Next Industrial Revolution* (Boston: Little, Brown, 2000), pp. 49–50.
4. This quotation has been attributed to J. Irwin Miller, former CEO of Cummins, Inc.
5. Michael A. Berry and Dennis A. Rondinelli, "Proactive Corporate Environmental Management: A New Industrial Revolution," *Academy of Management Executive* 12 (1998): 39.
6. Philip K. Howard, *The Death of Common Sense* (New York: Warner Books, 1994), p. 7.
7. This section has been adapted in part from Jethro K. Lieberman and George J. Siedel, *Business Law and the Legal Environment,* 3rd ed. (Orlando, FL: Harcourt Brace Jovanovich, 1992), pp. 724–731. The EPA Web site, http://www.epa.gov/, includes a section titled "Laws and Regulations" (September 12, 2001).
8. EPA, "The Plain English Guide to the Clean Air Act." Available online: http://www.epa.gov/oar/oaqps/peg_caa/pegcaa02.html (September 12, 2001).
9. EPA, "Toxic Substance Control Act." Available online: http://www.epa.gov/region5/defs/html/tsca.htm (September 12, 2001).
10. George J. Siedel, *Real Estate Law,* 3rd ed. (St. Paul, MN: West, 1993), p. 433.
11. EPA, "Endangered Species Act." Available online: http://www.epa.gov/region5/defs/html/esa.htm (September 12, 2001).

12. EPA, "Oil Pollution Act of 1990." Available online: http://www.epa.gov/region5/defs/html/opa.htm (September 12, 2001).

13. Congressional Research Service, *Summaries of Environmental Laws Administered by the Environmental Protection Agency* (Washington, DC: Congressional Research Service, 1997), p. 4.

14. Jingzhou Tao, "Environmental Liability of Foreign Invested Enterprises in the People's Republic of China," *International Business Lawyer* (July/August 2000): 314.

15. David J. Hayes and Judith E. King, "Nations Take Stricter Action on Environment," *National Law Journal* (February 7, 1994): 32.

16. C. Leigh Anderson and Robert A. Kagan, "Adversarial Legalism and Transaction Costs: The Industrial-Flight Hypothesis Revisited," *International Review of Law and Economics* 20 (2000): 6.

17. EPA, "Introduction to Laws and Regulations." Available online: http://www.epa.gov/epahome/lawintro.htm (September 12, 2001).

18. George J. Siedel (ed.), *The Lawyer and Business* (St. Paul, MN: West, 1976), pp. 97–100 (reprinted from Joseph C. Goulden, *The Superlawyers* (New York: Weybright and Talley, 1972).

19. Colleen Graffy, "Big Mac Bites Back," *ABA Journal* (August 1997): 22; "McLibel Two Take UK Government to Euro-court." Available online: http://www.mcspotlight.org/media/press/releases/msc200900.html (September 12, 2001).

20. *U.S.* v. *Hanousek,* 176 F.3d 1116 (1998).

21. Stephen B. Goldberg, Frank E. A. Sander, and Nancy H. Rogers, *Dispute Resolution: Negotiation, Mediation, and Other Processes* (New York: Aspen Law & Business, 1999), pp. 501–502.

22. EPA, "Negotiated Rulemaking." Available online: http://www.epa.gov/stakeholders/history.htm (January 2, 2001).

23. "Business advantages accrue to the companies that take the right steps to . . . manage how worldwide environmental issues affect them." S. Noble Robinson, Ralph Earle III, and Ronald A. N. McLean, "Transnational Corporations and Global Environment Policy," *Prism* (First Quarter 1994): 57.

24. Berry and Rondinelli, "Proactive Corporate Environmental Management," p. 41.

25. Matthew B. Arnold and Robert M. Day, *The Next Bottom Line: Making Sustainable Development Tangible* (Washington, DC: World Resources Institute, 1998), pp. 22–23.

26. Harry M. Carey Jr., "Environmental Auditing: One Lawyer's Perspective," *ACCA DOCKET* (Winter 1987): 17.

27. EPA, "Help on Compliance." Available online: http://www.epa.gov/reinvent/industry/help.htm (January 2, 2001).

28. National Conference of State Legislatures, "State Environmental Audit Laws and Policies: An Evaluation." Available online: http://www.ncsl.org/programs/esnr/auditsum.htm (September 12, 2001).

29. EPA, "Leveling the Playing Field: Eliminating the Economic Benefit of Violating Environmental Laws." Available online: http://es.epa.gov/oeca/models/lvlfield.html (September 12, 2001).

30. EPA and U.S. Department of Energy, *Environmental Management Systems Primer for Federal Facilities* (Washington, DC: EPA and U.S. Department of Energy, 1998), pp. 1, 22.

31. Ronald Begley, "Is ISO 14000 Worth It?" *Journal of Business Strategy* (September-October 1996): 53.

32. ISO, "ISO 14000." Available online: http://www.iso.ch/iso/en/iso9000–14000/iso14000/iso14000index.html (September 12, 2001).

33. ANSI, "Frequently Asked Questions." Available online: http://web.ansi.org/public/iso14000/faq_3.html (September 12, 2001).

34. ISO 14000 Information Center, "GM Requires Suppliers to Achieve ISO 14001 Certification by 2002." Available online: http://www.iso14000.com/WhatsNew/News01.htm (September 12, 2001).

35. Commission for Environmental Cooperation, "Improving Environmental Performance and Compliance: 10 Elements of Effective Environmental Management Systems." Available online: http://www.cec.org/files/PDF/LAWPOLICY/guide-e_EN.pdf (September 12, 2001).

36. *U.S.* v. *Bestfoods,* 118 S. Ct. 1876 (1998). The company referred to in the text as CPC later changed its name to Bestfoods.

37. Berry and Rondinelli, "Proactive Corporate Environmental Management," p. 41.

38. "3M Environmental Progress Report." Available online: http://www.mmm.com/profile/envt/manage.html (January 6, 2001).

39. Forest L. Reinhardt, "Environmental Product Differentiation: Implications for Corporate Strategy," *California Management Review* 40 (1998): 44.

40. Gladwin, "A Call for Sustainable Development," p. 3.

41. DuPont, "From the Chief Executive." Available online: http://www.dupont.com/corp/environment/comment.html (January 5, 2001).

42. Dow Jones, "Sustainability Group Index." Available online: http://www.sustainability-index.com/sustainability/investments.html (September 12, 2001).

43. Arnold and Day, *The Next Bottom Line,* p. 2.

44. Patagonia, "Environmental Grants." Available online: http://www.patagonia.com/enviro/enviro_grants.shtml (September 12, 2001).

45. "DuPont's Punt," *Economist* (October 2, 1999): 75.

46. Michael E. Porter, *Competitive Advantage* (New York: Free Press, 1985), p. 11.

47. World Business Council, "Eco-efficiency: Creating More Value with Less Impact." Available online: http://www.wbcsd.ch/newscenter/reports/2000/EEcreating.pdf (September 12, 2001).

48. World Business Council, "Eco-efficiency," p. 5.

49. Arnold and Day, *The Next Bottom Line,* pp. 19–39.

50. Arnold and Day, *The Next Bottom Line,* pp. 7–18.

51. Amory B. Lovins, L. Hunter Lovins, and Paul Hawken, "A Road Map for Natural Capitalism," *Harvard Business Review* (May-June, 1999): 145–158.

52. Lovins, Lovins, and Hawken, "Road Map," p. 146.

53. Berry and Rondinelli, "Proactive Corporate Environmental Management," p. 42.

54. Robert D. Klassen, "The Impact of Environmental Technologies on Manufacturing Performance," *Academy of Management Journal* 42 (1999): 613.

55. Arnold and Day, *The Next Bottom Line,* p. 27.

56. Hawken, Lovins, and Lovins, *Natural Capitalism,* p. 127.

57. Lovins, Lovins, and Hawken, "Road Map," p. 148.

58. William McDonough and Michael Braungart, "The Next Industrial Revolution," *Atlantic Monthly* (October 1998): 88–90.

59. John Carey, "When Green Begets Green," *Business Week* (November 10, 1997): 102.

60. "Greening the Government Through Waste Prevention, Recycling, and Federal Acquisitions," *Federal Register* 63 (1998): 49643.

61. EPA, "Environmentally Preferable Purchasing." Available online: http://www.epa.gov/opptintr/epp/aboutpage.htm (September 12, 2001).

62. EPA, "Environmentally Preferable Purchasing."

63. Sonoco, "Reduce, Reuse, Recycle." Available online: http://www.sonoco.com/reduce.htm (January 5, 2001).

64. Arnold and Day, *The Next Bottom Line,* pp. 29, 31.

65. "DuPont's Punt," *Economist* (October 2, 1999): 76.

66. Lovins, Lovins, and Hawken, "Road Map," 154.

67. 1999 CERES Report for Interface, Inc. Available online: http://www.interfaceinc.com/us/company/sustainability/frontpage.asp (September 12, 2001): 51.

68. Arnold and Day, *The Next Bottom Line,* p. 30.

69. Arnold and Day, *The Next Bottom Line,* p. 12.

70. Arnold and Day, *The Next Bottom Line,* p. 48.

71. Geoffrey Heal, "Environmental Disaster: Not All Bad News," *Financial Times* (October 30, 2000 supplement): 13.

72. "Profitability Meets the Environment," *Dividend* (Fall 1999): 17.

73. Lovins, Lovins, and Hawken, "Road Map," 155.

74. Gregory Dunn, "Enviro-Capitalists," *Religion and Liberty* (May-June 1998). Available online: http://www.acton.org/publicat/randl/98may_jun/dunn.html (September 12, 2001).

75. "Full Cost Accounting." Available online: http://www.dnr.state.wi.us/org/caer/cea/publications/pubs/co_048.htm (September 12, 2001).

76. EPA, "Small Business Waste Reduction Guide." Available online: http://es.epa.gov/new/business/sbdc/sbdc21.htm (September 12, 2001).

77. World Business Council for Sustainable Development, "WBCSD Platform for Corporate Eco-efficiency Performance." Available online: http://www.wbcsd.org/ee/EEMprofiles/index.htm (December 27, 2000).

78. CERES, "About CERES." Available online: http://www.ceres.org/about/index.html (January 6, 2001).

Chapter Five

1. Antonia Handler Chayes, Bruce C. Greenwald, and Maxine Paisner Winig, "Managing Your Lawyers," *Harvard Business Review* (January-February 1983): 84.
2. Michael A. Hitt, R. Duane Ireland, and Robert E. Hoskisson, *Strategic Management: Competitiveness and Globalization,* 2nd ed. (St. Paul, MN: West, 1997), pp. 95, 97–98.
3. Margery Gordon, "Execs Like You Better," *Corporate Counsel* (July 2001): 24.
4. Christy Eidson and Melissa Master, "Who Makes the Call?" *Across the Board* (March 2000): 16.
5. Mike France, "GE Shines as In-House Innovator," *National Law Journal* (April 17, 1995): C1.
6. Darlene Ricker, "The Vanishing Hourly Fee," *ABA Journal* (March 1994): 69. This article describes the first four alternatives in greater detail.
7. Laurel-Ann Dooley, "Law Firm 'Beauty Contests' Lose Allure as Companies Turn to RFPs," *Corporate Law Weekly* (November 25, 1999): 854.
8. John J. Marquess, "Legal Fee Audits: A Cost Control Primer," *Risk Management* (February 1999): 29.
9. Bob Van Voris, "Wal-Mart's Penny-Wise Lawyering," *Corporate Counsel* (October 1999): 34.
10. Van Voris, "Wal-Mart's Penny-Wise Lawyering," p. 30.
11. Van Voris, "Wal-Mart's Penny-Wise Lawyering," p. 34.
12. "Role of the General Counsel," *ACCA DOCKET* (September-October 1995): 60, 62.
13. Paul R. Rice, "Corporate Attorney-Client Privilege: Study Reveals Corporate Agents Are Uninformed; What They Don't Know Can Destroy the Privilege." Available online: http://www.acca.com/vl/privilege/rice.html (October 18, 1998).
14. "Ask the General Counsel," *ACCA DOCKET* (January-February 1996): 39.

15. "Ask the General Counsel," p. 39.

16. "Ask the General Counsel," p. 42.

17. Lawyers in the Trenches," *LD21* (Spring 2001): 16; "People Like Us," *LD21* (Spring 2001): 29.

18. "Ask the General Counsel," p. 42.

19. Robert S. Banks, "Companies Struggle to Control Legal Costs," *Harvard Business Review* (March-April 1983): 168.

20. "The Reengineering Process: Two Case Histories," *ACCA DOCKET* (September-October 1995): 20. The summary of the development of the DuPont Legal Model is drawn from this article.

21. Daniel B. Mahoney, "When Pruning Is in Order," *Business Law Today* (July-August 1996): 50.

22. Thomas L. Sager, "Toward a Common Goal," *ACCA DOCKET* (July-August 1997): 13. This article describes the first four elements of the DuPont plan.

23. "The Reengineering Process," p. 24.

24. Thomas L. Sager and Gerard G. Boccuti, "Achieving the Common Goal: DuPont's Performance Metrics," *ACCA DOCKET* (September-October 1997): 20–21.

25. Mahoney, "When Pruning Is in Order," p. 14.

26. Mahoney, "When Pruning Is in Order," pp. 16, 18.

27. Paul M. Barrett, "Tiny Firm Prospers Paring Fees DuPont's Way," *Wall Street Journal* (December 31, 1997): B1.

28. Mark Voorhees, "Learning the Law with a Mouse," *National Law Journal* (November 22, 1999): B10.

29. "Getting in Shape," *LD21* (Spring 2001): 7; "Dawn of the Machine Age," *LD21* (Spring 2001): 25; "Virtual Competition," *LD21* (Spring 2001): 28.

30. "GE and the Art of 'Systematic Common Sense,'" *Corporate Counsel* (August 2000): 51.

31. "The Profit Center," *LD21* (Spring 2001): 16.

32. Stephen E. Nowland, "The Law Department . . . Transformed," *LD21* (Spring 2001): 4.

33. Kevin G. Rivette and David Kline, "Discovering New Value in Intellectual Property," *Harvard Business Review* (January-February 2000): 58.

34. Catherine Aman, "The Money of Invention," *Corporate Counsel* (May 1999): 46.
35. Rivette and Kline, "Discovering New Value in Intellectual Property," p. 56.
36. Dennis Kneale, "Tylenol, the Painkiller, Gives Rivals Headaches in Stores and in Court," *Wall Street Journal* (September 2, 1982): 1.
37. Ellen Rodgers and Alan Ratliff, "Increasing Shareholder Value in the New Economy," *ACAA DOCKET* (November-December 2000): 62.
38. Aman, "The Money of Invention," p. 38.
39. "Trademarks," *Outside Counsel* (Summer 1994): 2–3.
40. Pamela L. Moore, "For Sale: Great Ideas, Barely Used," *Business Week* (April 3, 2000): 80.
41. Kevin G. Rivette and David Kline, *Rembrandts in the Attic: Unlocking the Hidden Value of Patents* (Boston: Harvard Business School Press, 2000).
42. Rivette and Kline, "Discovering New Value in Intellectual Property," p. 54.
43. "The Profit Center," *LD21* (Spring 2001): 17. See also Julie L. Davis and Suzanne S. Harrison, *Edison in the Boardroom: How Leading Companies Realize Value from Their Intellectual Assets* (New York: Wiley, 2001).
44. Aman, "The Money of Invention," p. 46.
45. Rivette and Kline, "Discovering New Value in Intellectual Property," p. 56.
46. Aman, "The Money of Invention," p. 44.
47. Jack L. Foltz, "Laws of Reality," *ACCA DOCKET* (May-June 1996): 48.
48. Catherine Aman, "What CEOs Really Think of GCs," *Corporate Counsel* (November 2000): 23.
49. Karen Hall, "What Would Ben Do?" *Corporate Counsel* (March 2001): 58.
50. Hall, "What Would Ben Do?" pp. 58–62. This article includes the summary of Heineman's accomplishments.
51. Hall, "What Would Ben Do?" p. 58.
52. This example is adapted from George J. Siedel, "The Decision Tree: A Method to Figure Litigation Risks," *Bar Leader* (January-February 1986): 18.

53. David Hechler, "GE's Juggling Act," *National Law Journal* (July 23, 2001): A16.
54. Thomas D. Cavenagh, *Business Dispute Resolution* (Cincinnati, OH: West Legal Studies in Business, 2000), p. 186.
55. Center for Public Resources, *Corporate Dispute Management 1982* (New York: Bender, 1982), p. 338.
56. George J. Siedel, "The Use of Mini-Trials to Resolve Construction Disputes," in *Construction Conflict Management and Resolution,* edited by Peter Fenn and Rod Gameson (London: E & FN SPON, 1992), p. 356.
57. Max Bazerman, *Judgment in Managerial Decision Making* (New York: Wiley, 1998), p. 129.
58. Catherine Cronin-Harris, *Building ADR Into the Corporate Law Department: ADR Systems Design* (New York: CPR Institute of Dispute Resolution, 1997), pp. 105–107.
59. Kenneth Glasner, "Contract Disputes: The Role of ADR," *Dispute Resolution Journal* (August-October 2000): 54.
60. William L. Ury, Jeanne M. Brett, and Stephen B. Goldberg, *Getting Disputes Resolved: Designing Systems to Cut the Costs of Conflict* (San Francisco: Jossey-Bass, 1988): 42.
61. Danny Ertel, "Turning Negotiation into a Corporate Capability," *Harvard Business Review* (May-June 1999): 61.
62. Thomas Donaldson, "Adding Corporate Ethics to the Bottom Line," *Financial Times* (November 13, 2000 supplement): 4.
63. Lynn Sharp Paine, "Does Ethics Pay?" *Business Ethics Quarterly* (2000), p. 34.
64. Jeffrey M. Kaplan, "Why Daiwa Bank Will Pay $340 Million Under the Sentencing Guidelines," ETHIKOS (May-June 1996): 1.
65. KPMG, *2000 Organizational Integrating Survey* (2000): 4.
66. Arthur Andersen, *Ethical Concerns and Reputation Risk Management* (1999): 12.
67. Linda Klebe Trevino, Gary R. Weaver, David G. Gibson, and Barbara Ley Toffler, "Managing Ethics and Legal Compliance: What Works and What Hurts," *California Management Review* 41 (1999): 135.
68. Lynn Sharp Paine, "Managing for Organizational Integrity," *Harvard Business Review* (March-April 1994): 113.

69. Trevino, Weaver, Gibson, and Toffler, "Managing Ethics and Legal Compliance," p. 137.
70. Paine, "Managing for Organizational Integrity," p. 111.
71. Paine, "Managing for Organizational Integrity," p. 111.
72. Trevino, Weaver, Gibson, and Toffler, "Managing Ethics and Legal Compliance," p. 137.
73. John Gibeaut, "Getting Your House in Order," *ABA Journal* (June 1999): 69.
74. Gibeaut, "Getting Your House in Order," p. 66.
75. Calmetta Coleman, "As Thievery by Insiders Overtakes Shoplifting, Retailers Crack Down," *Wall Street Journal* (September 8, 2000): A1.
76. KPMG, *2000 Organizational Integrity Survey* (2000): 2.
77. Timothy L. Fort, "How Relationality Shapes Business and Its Ethics," *Journal of Business Ethics* 16 (1997): 177.
78. Arthur Andersen, *Ethical Concerns and Reputation Risk Management,* p. 36.
79. Trevino, Weaver, Gibson, and Toffler, "Managing Ethics and Legal Compliance," p. 145.
80. Gibeaut, "Getting Your House in Order," p. 70.
81. D. S. Kim, "Safety: The Ultimate in Caring for People," *Executive Safety News* (1997). Available online: http://www.Dupont.com/safety/esn97–4/safecare.html (October 5, 2001).
82. Center for Public Resources, *Corporate Dispute Management 1982,* p. xxviii.
83. Thomas J. Peters, *In Search of Excellence* (New York: HarperCollins, 1983).
84. Jim Oliphant, "Florida Power Gets Expensive Lesson in Corporate Sensitivity," *Corporate Law Weekly* (May 13, 1999): 28.
85. Oliphant, "Florida Power," p. 28.
86. "Solzhenitsyn: Decline of the West," *Time* (June 19, 1978): 33.

The Author

George J. Siedel is Williamson Family Professor of Business Administration at the University of Michigan Business School. Professor Siedel received his B.A. degree from the College of Wooster, J.D. degree from the University of Michigan, and a Diploma in Comparative Legal Studies from Cambridge University, where he was a Ford Foundation fellow.

Professor Siedel has been admitted to practice before the U.S. Supreme Court and in Michigan, Ohio, and Florida. Following graduation from law school, he worked as an attorney in a professional corporation. He has also served on several boards of directors and as associate dean of the University of Michigan Business School. Prior to his appointment to the Williamson Family Professorship, professor Siedel held a University of Michigan Thurnau professorship.

Professor Siedel is the chief editor of the *Michigan Real Property Review* and has served as staff and special editor of the *American Business Law Journal*. The author of numerous books and articles, he has received several research awards, including the Faculty Recognition Award from the University of Michigan and the Hoeber Award from the Academy of Legal Studies in

Business. The Center for International Business Education and Research selected a case written by professor Siedel for its annual International Case Writing Award.

Professor Siedel has served as visiting professor of business law at Stanford University, visiting professor of business administration at Harvard University, and Parsons Fellow at the University of Sydney. He has been elected a Visiting Fellow at Cambridge University's Wolfson College and a Life Fellow of the Michigan State Bar Foundation. As a Fulbright Scholar, professor Siedel has also held a Distinguished Chair in the Humanities and Social Sciences.

Index